LIFE
as an Orphan
An encounter with God

GUERLINE CHARLES JEFFERS

Copyright © 2014 by Guerline Charles Jeffers

Life as an Orphan
An encounter with God
by Guerline Charles Jeffers

Printed in the United States of America

ISBN 9781498416467

All rights reserved solely by the author. The author guarantees all contents are original and do not infringe upon the legal rights of any other person or work. No part of this book may be reproduced in any form without the permission of the author. The views expressed in this book are not necessarily those of the publisher.

Scripture quotations are taken from the King James Version (KJV) – public domain

www.xulonpress.com

TABLE OF CONTENTS

Dedication vii

Life as an Orphan 9
   Three angels sent From God 12

Finally Independent 21

New Life in Christ 29
   Man looks at the outward appearance 34
   A Friend that's closer than a brother 46

My First Visitation 51

Being Led by the Holy Spirit 55
   Reunited 61
   A new plan 64
   Is it God? 66
   It was God! 72

The Beginning of Our Trials 77
   Detour on the road to Texas 85

Alone in the Lone Star State 87
   God will see you through 96

Words of Encouragement 101

DEDICATION

First of all I give honor, praise, and thanksgiving to the Lord Jesus Christ; through him all things have been made possible. I want to dedicate this book in honor of the Holy Spirit, who has guided me and enlightened my every thought to write every word of this book. I love you, Lord!

Second of all, I want to dedicate this book in honor of my husband who has received the instructions from the Lord for this book to be written and to be published. Mitchell, thank you for being an inspiration and for supporting me while writing this book. Thank you for our wonderful marriage. I love you!

Third of all, I want to dedicate this book in honor of the Singletons, my missionary family. I thank God for the big part you both have played in my life. Thank you for raising me up in the way that I should go in the Lord. It is a privilege and big accomplishment to know that your labor in the Lord wasn't in vain. I love you all and may God bless you!

LIFE AS AN ORPHAN

My story begins in Port-au-Prince, Haiti. I'm from a province called Port-de-Paix (Port of Peace). I'm known by those who know me as Lina. I remember having three brothers. The two youngest ones were twins. I didn't know too much about my biological mother, because I was very young when I was separated from her. I remember my biological father had such a love for me; I think he knew that I was a chosen child. I never understood why my father took me to an orphanage. For a long time I've wondered: Why am I here? Why has my father forsaken me? Doesn't he love me? Although he would come and visit me every Sunday, that wasn't enough for a lost little girl like me. I wanted to live with my father until the time had come for me to get married, but I was wrong—the Lord had a bigger plan for my life of which I had no knowledge.

My father took me to the first orphanage when I was five years old. It was being run by a man named Mr. Massoux; he was a doctor. I think he did the best he could to take care of all of us. There were times in which we went without food and water, but I can remember there was this particular woman of God, a worker in the orphanage; even from a very young age I could tell when this woman prayed, God moved immediately. I had no idea what prayer was, but truckloads of all kinds of food arrived to the orphanage when this woman prayed. I witnessed the power of prayer.

I remember living in that orphanage for a few years. The orphanage began to shut down slowly when Massoux's mother died unexpectedly. I think it took a toll on him; he suddenly changed his plans and decided not to continue running the orphanage anymore. He announced to all of us that the orphanage would be shutting down, and said that he was going to take every one of us to our biological parents. That night I had a vision; I saw all the kids of the orphanage along with the grown-ups who worked there lying outside on the ground, paralyzed in their left legs. They each had a long, open cut going down the side of their legs. I was down on the ground also but to my surprise, when I looked at my leg it wasn't cut. Till this day I can't tell what this vision represented, but what I saw was so vivid. I really think that God was trying to get my attention at a very early age.

The day finally came when Mr. Massoux began to take each of us back home to our parents. The trip took many days, because he couldn't take everyone home all at once; some lived far in the country and some lived nearby; we all lived in different locations.

I was very happy to know that I was going to be reunited with my father again. A girl named Patty and I were the last two girls left to be taken home. My great disappointment came when I thought Mr. Massoux was supposed to take both of us home, but instead he took us both to a social service office, a place for children. He told us that he would be back, but he never did come back for us. Psalms 118:8 says, "It is better to take refuge in the LORD than to trust in man."

Back then, I believed everything people had said to me. Do you know why? Because I was an only a child and I had no knowledge in the Word of God. I really didn't know who God was, or even if there was a God. For many years I've blamed Mr. Massoux for causing the disconnection between me and my father, but today I have come to a full understanding that it was part of God's plan for my life. He allowed it to happen this way. This is why in the book of Isaiah, God said, "For my thoughts are not your thoughts, and your ways are not my ways." His ways are higher than our ways and our thoughts. Sometimes things seem so unfair in the way that they play out in our lives, but God is in it and He has a plan.

Mr. Massoux never mentioned anything to the people where he had dropped us off. He simply dropped us off and left. We were there from some time in the morning until the middle of the afternoon unattended. I think one of the CPS workers noticed when Mr. Massoux had brought us to the place. She came outside and asked both Patty and I what we were doing there. We explained to her that the man who had brought us here told us to tarry there a little while until he came back for us. She gazed upon us sadly and said, "Mr. Massoux will not be coming back." Her name was Ms. Caretta; she told us that Mr. Massoux had nowhere to take us and he knew that this place would take care of us. I didn't get it. This man knew my father; why didn't he take me home? Again, this was beyond my understanding, but God had a plan.

Ms. Caretta told us that she knew of a place where we could stay for a couple of weeks, and then she would come back for us and take us to another orphanage. She took us to the place, and after she had dropped us off she reminded us again that she would be back. An overwhelming feeling came over me after she had left. I wasn't happy. I felt so uncomfortable being in that place; the atmosphere was different, and they were all grown kids. I felt out of place. I couldn't wait for the end of the two weeks to come. She came back after two weeks just as she had promised, and I was happy to see her again. I was glad to leave that place.

Ms. Caretta took us to another orphanage that was being operated by a lady name Mene. Mene had come from a different country; her orphanage was situated in the capital of Port-au-Prince. This woman had never married. She lived a single life, raising orphans just like me. When I got to her orphanage, I felt a little relief, because there were some kids there who were my age.

She put me and Patty, Rosa and three other small kids in a regular bedroom inside the house, because we were the five youngest kids among all of the others. I can't give you a full description of Mene because of the short length of time that I lived in her orphanage. One thing I can say: she was very wealthy and she was kind of evil. She had houses, land and properties as far as your eyes could see, but she lived in one of the homes she owned and had gathered all of us into one small place, which was her front porch.

She raised us like animals; the only times we would have shelter was when the night had come for us to lay our heads. She would open her front porch and she would tell the bigger kids to make the beds for the others to come and lay their heads on. Although she had all kinds of bunk beds and blankets in different houses on the same property, she wouldn't let the kids use them, because she was afraid that we would wet the mattresses and she'd have to replace them with new ones. Here's this woman who was probably the wealthiest one in that town, and was more careful about her beds and everything else than the orphans' lives.

The Bible said not to put our trust in our riches and Jesus also said in Matthew 16:26, "For what is a man profited, if he shall gain the whole world, and lose his own soul?...Or what shall a man give in exchange for his soul?" Mene was a great example of this scripture. She didn't live for the Lord, and she spent her whole life living for the devil. At times she would have rituals and we would partake with her, not knowing what this celebration meant. I used to think it was a regular party. I didn't know what all this meant and I also didn't know about the devil and the satanic realm.

I think Mene was 81 years old when she died. She died from the shocking news coming directly from the White House in Port-au-Prince. At that time "Baby Doc" was in office, but he was overpowered by a group of bandits who had forced him to leave the White House unexpectedly; ever since then Haiti was never the same. I think Mene had more than a connection with the President. As a result of the bad news, she deteriorated, went through a trauma and died.

Three angels sent from God
The night before her death, there came a woman to her house from the same country and her name was Ms. Good. Ms. Good was a woman of God and she loved the Lord dearly. Until this day, she is still about the Lord's business; she has a big orphanage outside the capital of Port-au-Prince. After Mene's death, I really think that God brought Ms. Good there just in time to oversee the orphanage and take care of us. Ms. Good had a big heart and I could tell she really did love us all. The day after she arrived, she moved all of us to her home. Although her house wasn't big enough to fit all of us, she did the best she could. I'm pretty sure that the Lord was pleased with her.

At that time there was an American couple who came for a visit while we were still at Mene's orphanage; I think the Lord already knew that we were going to be with Ms. Good for an appointed time. Ms. Good wasn't usually there, because she was on missions trips most of the time; she didn't really have the time to be with us. She was a missionary. She did leave someone in her stead to care for us while she was gone. She was a single mother and she did a pretty good job. The American couple was Mr. and Mrs. Singleton; they came back for the second time and stayed at Ms. Good's place, where we all were. They also had a one year old daughter named Ferra.

The Singleton's were also missionaries; they stayed there for a while during Ms. Good's absence. We had all gotten acquainted with them and we also fell in love with them. This also was part of God's plan, because they were going to be the next providers for us. When Ms. Good came back from her trips she would bring us new clothes and shoes and all kinds of goodies. We loved her so much and she knew it; that's how we showed her our appreciation. Now I'm not saying we didn't give her some hard times — because we did, bless her heart — but she understood, because that's what kids do.

Ms. Good was also in charge of a Christian summer camp located outside the capital. I always enjoyed going to summer camp every year, because I had learned so many things, especially about the Lord.

Ms. Good also noticed how attached we were to the Singleton's. She made a statement and said that we were better off to be with them instead of her, because she could tell how much we loved them rather than her. All I can say is that this too was part of God's plan.

I know that everything happens for a reason. I know that the Lord had called the Singletons to take over the orphanage at this set time. Thank God for all these great people, whether good or bad, who obeyed the Lord and made it happen for all of us. I'm so thankful.

I believe I was about 7 or 8 years old when the Singletons took over the orphanage. They had rented a big house with two floors. There were many bedrooms, bathrooms, living rooms, and all kind of rooms. It was located in the city. They moved us all in, including their one year old daughter. Altogether, we were 19 kids. They named the orphanage The House of Blessings. For the first time in my adolescent life, I was happy; I had a lot of joy. I felt right at home.

I loved the environment, great neighborhood, and friendly people everywhere. After a rough ride, I was somewhat comforted. The Singletons were very good to us, especially me. They taught us a lot of good things.

After we were all established in that big house, the Singletons engaged themselves in more important things. They hired two workers to help in the orphanage. They got us into new schools; we also had a new church which we attended every Sunday. I remember Mr. Singleton would come downstairs every Sunday making sure that we all went to church, because some of the kids would pretend to be sick so they wouldn't have to go to church. We were each assigned to a sponsor, and our sponsors did a very good job.

Christmas season was so special to me; we used to receive a lot of gifts from our sponsors and from other churches of God. The Singletons gave so much to us; we had plenty of fun playing all kinds of interesting games. Not only did they give me an academic education, but also a Christian education.

At nighttime we would gather together in one place to have devotions, we would sing praise and worship songs and praise the Lord. We would also read the Word of God. They would challenge us to memorize Bible scriptures and we'd receive a prize for it; they made learning very easy and fun. They even taught me how to speak English. Ms. Singleton taught me how to cross-stitch, and how to make all kinds of arts and crafts. They both were very gifted in different areas and still are. I can say that I was their favorite and some of the other kids didn't like it.

Today, I've learned that it was the favor of the Lord upon my life and His favor is still upon me. I didn't do anything to inherit it, neither did I deserve it, but by the grace of God I am what I am. I found favor with the Singletons; I was always with them when they went different places. They took me almost everywhere they went. When they would go out to eat, they would allow me — out of all the kids — to go upstairs and babysit their one year-old daughter. It used to be so much fun watching her.

God granted me access to them. The favor of the Lord was so strong upon my life, it even got to a point where adoption had almost taken place, but it didn't happen because it wasn't part of God's plan. I was so happy though, knowing that I was going to be part of their family, for once again I would have a real mom and dad. I believe that I'm still part of their family, as they're like a mother and a father to me. I love them just as much as I would love my own mother and father. I could say the kind of life that God had allowed them to give me was a gift.

I found out almost a year ago through a word of prophecy spoken over my life, that when I was three years old, my biological mother had planned to give me up to the devil, but thanks be to God who had placed his seal upon my forehead before I was even formed in my mother's womb. He knew me (Psalm 139:13). The enemy couldn't touch me, hallelujah! The Singletons did an outstanding job raising me, I love them very much and I thank God for them every day. They were two angels that God sent to Haiti at such a time.

They set up this new rule in the House of Blessings; we were given responsibilities and they also gave us an allowance. When we brought home good grades from school, they would always take us to this nice restaurant up in the mountain. I used to love going to this buffet, because it had all kinds of spicy and great tasting food. We used to get treats for everything we did well. The Singletons spent all their time helping us in everything; they knew each of us in particular.

I remember every Friday night we used to eat popcorn and watch a new movie. Every Friday was a movie night, and every Saturday was beach day. I used to love it. One thing was so hilarious; we used to soak in the sun just like the Singletons, not knowing later that our skin would get darker. I didn't understand. We were so united with them, deep down in our kid minds we thought we were white also; but today, even if I would get paid to do it again, I wouldn't do it.

We all had responsibilities; the Singletons put us into groups of four. Every week the first team would work in the kitchen, while the second team took care of the front and backyard; the third team would be responsible to clean inside the house and the fourth team would clean all the bathrooms. Each week, each team would take turns in different chores.

We weren't good kids all the time — some of us would get into trouble at times — but the Singletons weren't the type of parents who were out to get us. They gave so many warnings before they could exercise that paddle on us, but no matter how hard they tried, we still got to a point where we had to get paddled, but that's how we had learned not to do it again.

I used to love it when missionary teams would come from time to time to the orphanage to do maintenance work and build churches. They would accomplish a lot. By the time they left to go back to the states, we would all be crying and they would also be crying because we all had gotten so attached to one another in a short period of time. I had so much fun growing up.

I attended a French-speaking school until I was in the 8th grade. The Singletons had made me an offer to switch from a French-speaking school to an English-speaking school. I didn't see it coming, but I was happy about it. Mr. Singleton said I didn't have to switch schools if I didn't want to, but I kept thinking to myself, *What would the other kids say?* or *What would they do?* Sure enough, they didn't like it — some of them were jealous of me. I can understand how they felt, because I probably would have felt the same way if I were in their shoes, but I loved them anyway. Some said that I was the Singletons' favorite. I got persecuted a little bit, but I didn't let it move me, because God's presence was always with me and I knew His hand and His favor was upon me.

In spite of everything, I chose to attend the English-speaking school. The name was MSCA; it was run by married pastors named the Joy family. They were generous, kind-hearted people, who had a big heart for Haiti, and also owned a church. I used to attend their church when I first started going to their school. I also learned a lot about God through them.

I felt like I accomplished a lot during the three years that I went to their school. I was part of the cheerleading squad, I participated in the chapel service every Wednesday, and I brought in good grades all the time. The Singletons were very proud of me. I used to love Wednesdays, because the students used to have so much fun at chapel. One of my favorite times while attending the Joy's school was the lock-ins. The principal would have all of the high school students visit; they had a big home and we use to have so much fun.

I attended 3 years of high school at their location, and then I switched schools again in 1997 to a more private, small Christian school run by another missionary couple who were also pastors. They ran an orphanage with 8 boys, and they were one of our good neighbors.

I remember when we left Ms. Good's orphanage, all of our birth certificates were lost and the Singletons had another birth certificate and a passport made for me. Some years later, I found my real birth certificate. My new certificate date of birth was different, but the year was the same.

In the summer of 1995, I was 16 years old. I remember the Singletons took me to the U.S. Consulate and I was granted a tourist visa. I remember thanking the Lord for all His goodness. It was a miracle, and I was so thrilled. For the first time, the Singletons took me to the States.

When we arrived at the Miami airport, a small incident happened — I got lost in the check-in area. I was so intimidated by the greatness of America. It wasn't anything like to Haiti. Haiti is so small that one can find their way out at any time, but the States was different. I couldn't find my way out. I was looking for the Singletons while they were looking for me. I believe that they thought they had lost me, so I prayed and I asked the Lord to help me. All of a sudden, I heard my name called out of the intercom and I was directed to the baggage claim area where the Singletons were. I was so happy to reunite with them again; we all had a good laugh about it.

I was invited to an international youth convention that was held in Phoenix, Arizona. I got to represent Haiti's flag and it was an honor. I remember feeling very special in the eyes of God, because I knew that the Lord was behind everything that was happening in my life. I thank the Lord for the Singletons, because they have done far more beyond my expectations.

I remember it got so hot in Arizona that it was nothing like Haiti's climate. I also visited the Grand Canyon while I was in Phoenix; it was such a beautiful sight to behold, it was unreal. I was part of the youth team who worked at the Indian Reservation for about a week. We were so exhausted after each day was over. I enjoyed everything, because it was all new to me. After we left Arizona we took another flight to Lake Wales, FL. I was so amazed by the length and height of the buildings; everything was in order, the streets looked so clean and I had met a lot of good people. I was in the States for about a month and a half, and I had visited so many different states.

One of states that the Singletons took me to was Mississippi. Mr. Singleton was from Jackson. Mr. Singleton's parents were good to me, and I really enjoyed their cooking. I remember feeling kind of strange, though, while I was in Mississippi. After Mississippi, we went on to North Webster, Indiana. Mrs. Singleton was from Indiana. Mrs. Singleton also took me to her mother's house for some time, and I had a lot of fun riding with Mrs. Singleton's youngest sister to some interesting places. I really enjoyed the good times.

I also met a boy there who was interested in me. I didn't know how to react towards him, because I was inexperienced and very shy. He took me out one night to the fair; I remember we rode on some crazy, scary rides. Among the rides was a particular one named "The Zipper" according to him. It was all right for him because he was familiar to all of the rides at the fair; but as for me, I was screaming from the top of my lungs and I couldn't wait for the ride to stop. All he did was laugh hard. I got a little bit mad because he had set me up. After the night was over he took me home, but nothing happened between us. I told him that I had a very good time.... NOT! (Just kidding.)

After I had got back from the states, I remember thinking to myself that I wanted to go back again. I brought so many good memories with me. All the other kids were so eager to know how my trip went, so I sat down with them and I told them everything, and they were very happy because I had brought them each something to enjoy. The Singletons had really wanted to take the rest of the kids to the states to have an experience, but they couldn't afford it.

In the following summer of 1996, the Singletons took me back to the States for the second time. I was there for two weeks. Again, I had such a wonderful time. The Singletons now had two beautiful children of their own — Ferra and Troy. Troy was born three years later at a Haitian hospital. I remember his birth had brought so much joy and comfort to the Singletons' lives and to all of us, as well. We watched them grow in our presence and they were so much fun to have around.

The Singletons gave up their lives and their youth, and left everything else they had behind, not to mention all the persecutions, the critics and the lies that they have endured from other people just to fulfill God's plan in our lives. I'm very humbled. I know that God isn't through with them yet, because I can sense a great blessing from the Lord is awaiting them. I can't wait to rejoice with them once more.

In the beginning of 1994, I remember there had been a lot of political problems in Haiti. Haiti was a very unsafe place to be at that time, but nevertheless God was always watching over us. We've always been protected by the Almighty. Back when President Titid was in office, he put the country in so much trouble and he also deceived the Haitian people. He started off with a good start, but at the end of his second term, he took on a drastic change and turned for the worst. He was very wicked, according to what some people had protested against him. He raised a lot of rebels in the country and I remember he had eliminated all the military force. What is a country without an army? This had been one of the many questions raised by so many Haitian people to the president.

I had heard so many bad things about this man, and I was glad when God finally removed him from his position. There were times at school while we'd still be in class, and we would hear gun shots; not even one or two gun shots, but it would be massive shootings that lasted for hours.

I remember one of the workers at the orphanage that would come to pick us up from school. At times he wouldn't know what to do, because there were so many of us. He was like a Papa duck with so many little ducklings following behind him, but God would always make a safe way out for him so he could lead us back to the orphanage. There was always something wrong going on in Haiti at that time. There was not a day that went by when something wasn't stirred up, but I knew that God was in control.

Our country went through a period of embargo — nothing came in and nothing went out. I remember the gas prices had gotten really high and the price of food was very expensive. We went without food for a little while, but the Singletons would always create something on the menu in order for us to eat, even if there wasn't enough. Through the entire time of the embargo, the Singletons struggled so hard to keep us fed.

There was a time when the Singletons had to separate from the orphanage and moved to their own place in the mountains, yet still overseeing the orphanage. I remember they had picked me to come and stay with them; I was so happy and I felt so loved. I don't think they knew the issues that went on between me and the other kids, but there were so many pressures and tensions among some of the orphanage kids because of me. I know it was part of God's plan for the Singletons to treat me the way they did, and I was very grateful.

I remember we lived in that big house for about ten years. I had a lot of good memories; I think we all did. It was very disappointing when I found out that we had to move to a different place, because the owner of the house had decided that he wasn't going to rent his place anymore.

The Singletons had found another place for the orphanage; it was a little farther away than the first one. This house wasn't as big as the first one. The Singletons stayed on the second floor and there was only one room on the first floor, and because the boys were few that was the perfect spot for them. There were two separate small rooms outside the house. The Singletons put all the big girls into one room and the younger girls were in the other room. I think if the Singletons could have afforded to move us into a bigger place, or even moved us to a place the same size as the first orphanage, they would have done so. I suppose it was a lack of support from some churches of God and other organizations which were being diminished, and had no way to contribute.

We had another rule in the orphanage: every Saturday we were free to go out after we finished our chores. Also, we had a curfew; we had to get back to the house by six o'clock, before dark. Even after the Singletons moved the orphanage to this new location, it didn't stop us from visiting our old neighborhood from time to time.

Even though there were restrictions which prevented any of us from going back there, we still visited old friends. I think we lived in that house for about two years. There were so many transitions taking place in the orphanage at the time.

After two years, I found out that we were going to move out for the third time. It didn't really matter because I wasn't very fond of that place. This time we were leaving the city to go to the mountains. I believe when we moved to the mountains it was 1997. We moved to a new house. It wasn't painted, it had two floors, it wasn't very big, and it was somewhat similar to the previous house. The Singletons stayed on the second floor while we, the orphanage kids, stayed on the first floor.

I remember it felt so different living in the mountains. It was kind of a strange place to me; the atmosphere was different and it was too quiet. Also, the people were a bit strange, and their speech was different. The only thing I think I liked about the mountains was the weather; it was a lot cooler than it was in the city.

Thank God I only stayed there for a few years. I graduated from high school two years after we moved up to the mountains. In the summer of 1999, I received my high school diploma. I was so grateful to the Lord and to the Singletons for such an accomplishment in my life. I was so happy. I remember thinking: What is the next thing that God has in store for me? Sure enough, the Lord always has something prepared for every one of us to take onto the next step.

FINALLY INDEPENDENT

I remember the Singletons had found me a good job right after I graduated from high school; it was a teacher's assistant position at MSCA, the first English-speaking school that I went to. I was getting paid a fair amount, which was far more than I expected. It was a blessing from the Lord. The Singletons couldn't afford to send me to college, even though they had tried everything they could, but God still had a plan.

I remember the Singletons had told me that I needed to move out because I was old enough to take care of myself, which was fine with me, because I didn't favor the mountain at all. I remember one of the boys from the orphanage was told the same — that he also had to move out. We both were looking for a place to stay, but we couldn't find one. Finally our Haitian church pastor had heard that we were looking for a place to stay and suggested that we come and stay at his place for a little while until we could get back on our feet. We were so thankful.

I had started a relationship with a guy right after I had moved up to the mountains. By the time I moved back down to the city I had started another relationship with a different guy who was a police officer; it was a mess. I ended up leaving my first boyfriend (who was a Christian) to settle with the second guy I didn't know too well. Of course there was a lot of explanation required on my part, but I didn't have anything to say except that I was so immature. I wasn't in love with the second guy, either. I stayed with him because of my circumstances. I remember by Christmas time of 1999, our pastor had already mentioned that my orphanage brother and I should look for a different place to stay.

I was back to searching for a new place but I couldn't find one, as usual. I think I had mentioned it to my boyfriend and to my big surprise he told me that his mother was getting ready to rent a bigger house for the family, and he also said that there was room for me if I was interested. I didn't really have a choice. I was thinking, "I can't move in with this guy," because we had not married, but he was fine with it because he wasn't a Christian. This was one of the issues that I had against him. I was 21 years old when it all took place. We got engaged and I thought I was sending a message, but in reality I was still not married in the eyes of the church. I had always wanted to do what was right, but I had no options. I only had to use what was set before me.

I finally rented a room from my boyfriend's mother. It wasn't easy for me, but it was the only option that I had because I was young and I didn't really know how to go about things. However, that's how I have learned. The fact that I was living under the same roof as my boyfriend bothered me. I had no choice; I needed a place to stay. House hunting in Haiti wasn't easy and there wasn't a lot to work with. My boyfriend really wanted to get married, but something inside of me had kept me from accepting his proposal. I know it had to be the Lord telling me that I should wait because it wasn't the right time, or the right person.

I had another problem where I was late for work most of the time because I had lived too far from my job. The principal had gotten tired of me coming late all the time; she said if I didn't do something about it she would have to let me go, but I wasn't going to let that happen. I began to pray more that the Lord would open another door for me.

After a year went by, the Lord provided a new place for me which was five steps away from my job. My boyfriend didn't like it; we were already having some problems and I was glad to move away from him. I don't know why, but I felt like I was in bondage when I was with him. I felt relieved as soon as I left him.

My new place was a regular apartment which the landlord had divided into single rooms. There was another teacher already living in one of the rooms, so I wasn't alone. The owner of the apartment and his wife stayed downstairs. It was much easier for me to go to work and to move around. I was always on time. It was the best thing that the Lord did for me. My love life had been a roller coaster; I used to jump from one relationship to another. I can't remember being settled with any of them for more than a year. I was looking for something in particular in all of them, but I couldn't find it. I was looking for God in every single one of them, but the Lord was nowhere to be found.

When I started teaching kindergarten, it was back in the summer of 1999. I was so happy and I was so glad to be on my own. I had so much fun teaching the little kids because I really love kids. I think children are the most wonderful works of God. I worked with a teacher whose name was Pam. She was a very nice person and we were also roommates. She also had a heart for teaching and she loved kids. I had a blast. I taught kindergarten for five years and I don't know why, but I was getting tired of what I used to love doing. I believe it was the Lord that had put this feeling in my heart, and I think He was trying to tell me that there was more He required of me to do.

I remember two different occasions I tried to leave my job to do something different, but it wasn't the right time. I had applied for a U.S. visa in 2001 and I got denied. I tried it again two years after and I still got denied. It hurt me so bad; I questioned the Lord, "Why did I get denied these two times when I'd already been to the States before?" It didn't make sense to me. I remember saying to the Lord that I'd never set foot inside the U.S. consulate again, not unless He sent me. I meant that I would never apply for another foreign visa. What the Lord had wanted me to do was there, but it wasn't the right timing. There is a season for everything, and a time to every purpose under Heaven (Ecclesiastes 3:1).

Before I left my job, an incident happened. I had a vision about my boss and she was accusing me of something I didn't do. In my vision, our kindergarten class was getting ready to take their morning break. I was standing at the end of the line and the other teacher was standing in front of the line, but while we were on our way to go upstairs to the cafeteria, she decided to abandon the line and she went to chat with the secretary. The line broke out of rank, and the children were scattered everywhere and guess who the principal came to yell at? Me. However, the Lord had a plan and I didn't know it. I believe the Lord was preparing me for what was going to happen. The Lord also showed me that I was innocent, and the person that the principal really needed to yell at was the other teacher, but instead she came against me.

My vision came to pass a week later when I took my class to the playground. I would usually sit in a particular spot where I could supervise each and every student. I remember I had a book in my hand and I was kind of reading through it, when all of sudden there were two boys playing with the swings and they were trying to hit one another with the swings. It happened the moment I put my eyes in the book; it happened so quickly. While the principal passed by the doorway leading to the playground, she saw it. I could tell she was angry; she walked up to me just like in my vision and began to scream in my face, but I remember telling her that there was no need for her to be screaming like that. I like how the Holy Ghost operates; He doesn't hide anything from his servants. He will show it to you before it even happens (John 16:13).

In the middle of the year, 2004 my trial had begun. An overwhelming feeling came upon me and I knew immediately something was wrong. I knew it had to do with the principal, but didn't really know what it was all about. There was also an uneasy feeling that I've never felt before and I knew it wasn't a good one. It happened at the end of the school year in the summer of 2004, when the principal usually had a yearly teacher's evaluation. The Lord showed me that she had been holding something against me for two years and that she was bringing it to an end.

It came to pass on the day she had her teacher's evaluation, when it was my turn to go into her office. I could already see the devilish look on her face, and from the moment I had sat down on the seat she began to speak inappropriately; I mean her tone of voice was so wrong. I was prepared for what could've been my last year working for her. I remember I had never felt so embarrassed and so low in my life that I began to cry; I was so upset. After she was through with me, I noticed that the overwhelming feeling had been lifted off of me and I felt free from the inside.

For a long while, I had resentment against her because she had caused a bad wound in my heart. The bad thing was she meant evil against me, but on the positive side the Lord took what she meant to do for evil and turned it around for my good (Genesis 50:20). I told her that the Lord had revealed to me what was going on and that she was already exposed. I remember thinking to myself, "Isn't she supposed to be a pastor's wife? Where is the love?" God had allowed this to happen just to start His purpose in my life.

A week after that, I was coming from church when all of a sudden I heard the voice of the Lord for the first time. The Lord spoke to me and He said, "Why don't you go to Santo Domingo?" While I was still pondering these words, He spoke to me again and said, "Go to your friend Clarice and ask her for more information." I went to my friend Clarice just as I was told by the Lord. When I told her the word that the Lord had spoken to me, and I also let her know that the Lord wanted her to give me more information about Santo Domingo, I was very surprised by her answer. With a big smile on her face she said, "Girl, you came to the right person." At that time she was renting this apartment in Santo Domingo, and she told me to rent a room in her apartment for a month just to get familiar with the country and to get acquainted with some of the people. Then I really knew it was God who had spoken to me. I was very happy.

When I told some of my orphanage family about the drastic move that I was going to make in my life, they said it wasn't a good idea. They didn't really dwell on it because they thought I was not capable to take this big step on my own, but I had to obey the Lord. The Lord didn't allow me to dwell on it either, because all I felt was so much peace and joy. I can't recall the date or time when my friend Clarice came to my house to collect the rent money for the month that I had to stay at her apartment. I also paid her for electricity a week before I left for Santo Domingo.

I remember it was three of us together who had traveled that morning. There was another male teacher who came with us; he stayed at Clarice's apartment too, and he also had to pay for rent during his stay at her apartment. He was dating one of the elementary school teachers and his purpose was to come and have an engagement ring made for his lovely girlfriend. We traveled by bus and it took five to six hours to get there. When we finally arrived, we were all exhausted.

The funny thing is that when we got to her apartment, there was no electricity. Everybody around us had electricity but her. The other teacher and I were kind of puzzled, because we had paid for electricity. I decided to ask her, "why isn't there electricity in her apartment?" She said she was having trouble with her electric box. That was a big lie and she knew it, too. I think what had happened was that she didn't pay for her electric bills and the electric company had cut her power off. That was the first issue. Then, the next day we went with her to the grocery store and she looked at us and said, "Aren't you guys going to buy some groceries?"

The male teacher and I looked at each other again with a question mark on our faces. "Hello, we already paid you for everything before we got to your apartment, remember?" We didn't say anything and we kept our mouths shut just to avoid some arguments. That was my second issue with her, but I still loved her anyway. She lured me into buying a bed which I didn't think was necessary. I knew what she was trying to do; she wanted to keep my bed after I left to go back to Haiti. She got her wish though, but not for very long.

The next day, all three of us went out shopping. I had so much fun. I discovered so many wonderful places. Santo Domingo is a beautiful country; it is very big compared to Haiti. It is very organized and had mostly clean areas. The only thing that differentiates Haiti from Santo Domingo is the food. I love my Haitian cuisine; there's nothing like it. A lot of the people there were very friendly.

I remember while we were inside the mall, this Dominican guy walked up to me and began to speak in Spanish. I had no idea what he was saying to me—I didn't know any Spanish at the time. Although I had taken Spanish class in school, I didn't think it was enough for me to carry a full blown conversation. Another issue I had was that he spoke too fast. My friend started laughing because she knew Spanish and I didn't. She told the guy that I had no idea of what had been said, because I didn't speak Spanish. The man told her to translate for him. She told me in Creole that the guy was interested in me and would like to go out with me. She also told me that he seemed like a nice guy and I should give him a chance.

The first thing that I thought to do was to stop and think about it, but I felt like my friend was very pushy about it and I wasn't interested. Believe it or not, the Lord was in it. That was the very guy who became a guide to me after a month and a half later when I went back to Santo Domingo, and he appears again later in my story. His name was Ernesto.

A week after I stayed in Clarice's apartment, she left for Haiti and didn't even tell me. She had changed so much towards me. She had three kids of her own and was married to a man who used to be one of the school teachers, but because they were having problems in their marriage, she had decided to go to Santo Domingo and rent an apartment there for her and her kids. That is the reason why she was going back and forth to Haiti from Santo Domingo. She used to have a babysitter who stayed with her children during her absence. After she had left, there wasn't really much we could do because we didn't really have any directions to guide us. She used to take us to different places because she knew how to get around, since she had lived there for quite a while. Two days before we left her apartment I cooked dinner using the groceries that we had contributed to her house with our money, and everyone ate. I never thought that it was going to be an issue. The babysitter called Clarice on the phone and told several lies on me; the sad thing was that she believed her. I ended up staying for two weeks instead of one month.

When I got back from Santo Domingo, I was very discouraged. I knew that the Lord had never intended for my visit to end up the way it did. I also knew that it was the devil that was behind it all. The devil was trying to get me so discouraged to a point where I would get so fed up with Santo Domingo and never return there to receive what the Lord had for me. I began to pray and ask the Lord what had gone wrong. Wasn't He the one who had told me to go to Santo Domingo? What should I do now? The Lord answered me through a night vision and He said, "Go." I thanked the Lord for another confirmation because I knew it was His voice that I heard. I had set a date and time to go back to Santo Domingo.

This time I went there to stay until further notice from the Lord. In the meantime, some of my orphanage family was still wondering about my decision. A week after I went back to Santo Domingo, I received an awful phone call from Clarice. I didn't expect to hear from her. She was very rude, her words were hurtful, and she was wrong because she believed in a lie. I think the last thing she mentioned over the phone before she hung up was that she was keeping my bed, which I already suspected. It was premeditated, because she already knew what she was going to do from the beginning. I was thinking to myself that she could have it—I could always get a new one—but my friends told me not to let her have it because I was going to need it when I got back to Santo Domingo. It wasn't a big deal anyway because I had enough money saved up on my account.

NEW LIFE IN CHRIST

It was July 17, 2004 when I finally went back to Santo Domingo for good. Ernesto, my Dominican friend, had stayed in contact with me while I was still in Haiti. He knew which day I was coming back to the DR and he waited for me at the bus station. When I had got to the bus station I didn't see him, so I started to panic. I went to the customs area to get some information about him, but the people there didn't seem to know what I was talking about. I decided to wait a little while, but I thought to myself that if he didn't show up that I'd go ahead and get a taxi and go to a motel.

After a lot of run around, Ernesto finally showed up; I thanked the Lord. I was so happy that the Lord had sent me some help, because He knew that I was going to be in a strange country. Ernesto and I took another bus to go to the capital of Santo Domingo. He took me to his apartment; to be honest, it wasn't really what I had expected, but I was grateful that he was there to help me. I can understand why he was living in such a condition—it was because he had a poor job. Nothing happened between him and me in that apartment. He had a vacation from his job during my stay over his place. I tried to help him the best way I could.

I remember telling him that it was uncomfortable for me to stay in his apartment, because we were only friends. There was no running water in his place, so he had to carry the water in a bucket back and forth to the house so we could get cleaned up. The bucket part wasn't really something new to me because I used to do the same thing in Haiti in some places where I used to live. I told Ernesto that I wanted to rent my own apartment and he agreed to help me find one.

His vacation ended and he went back to work after I had been in his apartment for a week. I remember he took me to his sister's house every day so that I wouldn't be lonely in his house. He had introduced me to her and her children and I got acquainted with them. I would spend the day at his sister's, and when he came from work he would take me back to his apartment.

Ernesto's sister Sulu had four children and they were all grown young men. Her second oldest son, Miko, knew a little bit of English and Ernesto had asked him to help me find my way around. I felt relieved that I could express myself in a country where hardly anybody spoke any other language but Spanish. Ernesto found me an apartment and I moved out of his place two weeks later.

My apartment was in the same area as his sister's; we were close neighbors. His sister had also become a great help to me. She made sure that I got fed every day; she was a very good person. During my time at my new apartment, the Lord spoke to me and revealed things to me. He showed me that I was battling with unforgiveness. What happened between my former principal and me in Haiti had haunted me day after day. I held a grudge against her ever since I moved to Santo Domingo. My heart was wounded and I didn't know how to patch it. When I asked the Lord to help me, He hearkened unto my prayer. The Lord began to perform a work in me; it was amazing. He began to mend my heart and healed the scars.

After the Lord finished operating on me, He gave me a new heart. He taught me how to forgive despite the circumstance. I felt an immediate release in my heart. I was free, and instead of hate I felt love in my heart towards my former principal.

Right after that amazing change, the Lord showed me through a vision that I must go and make peace with her. I had promised that I would do it as soon as an opportunity presented itself.

If you're battling with unforgiveness, ask God to help you and He will be more than happy to deliver you. In Matthew 6:15, Jesus said, "If ye forgive not men their trespasses, neither will your Father forgive your trespasses." It doesn't matter who's right or who's wrong; the right thing to do is what the scriptures says: forgive so you can be forgiven. What matters to God is how you respond to every situation. I believe this was another reason why God sent me to Santo Domingo.

In the process of time, Miko had fallen in love with me and I remember telling him not to let that happen. Who can control love? Only God can. When Ernesto had found out that Miko and I were seeing each other he was mad, but I never had any feelings for him. Even though I tried, it just wasn't there.

Meanwhile, I was looking for a job. I had gone to three different companies and they told me that I needed to have a *cedula*. I had questioned myself, "What is a *cedula*?" Miko was waiting outside for me and when I came out I remember he asked me, "Did you get the job?" I told him that they said I needed a *cedula* in order to work for their company. Miko asked me, "What did I tell them?"

I said, "I told the manager that I can get a *cedula* tomorrow."

The manager was very surprised of my answer and he said, "Really? You mean you can get a *cedula* that quickly?" Furthermore, he said if I could bring my *cedula* then I could start working that following Monday. Silly me—I thought I knew everything.

A *cedula* is a residency card that every foreigner must have in order to work, just like it is in any other country. The way that the word *cedula* sounded in Spanish, anybody who speaks English would think that it meant "cellular" in English. Well, that's what I thought. Miko tried to warn me about it, but I didn't listen.

Here's the catch; I came home that afternoon and I went and bought a used cell phone, but Miko kept warning me about getting the wrong thing. Maybe if he had been in the interview with me, he could have probably convinced me so that I wouldn't have made this terrible mistake. Just like the proverb says, "You learn by your own mistakes." It was good that I had learned a new word in Spanish, but the outcome was very disappointing.

I went back to the company that Monday morning with a big smile on my face. I talked to the secretary and I explained to her that I was told to have a *cedula* in order to start working there. She asked me to bring it out. This time Miko was standing there with me and I could hear him say, "No, not the cellular." Still, I was confident that this was what they wanted. Finally, when I reached down into my purse and I brought my cellular out, the secretary said something I wasn't ready to hear.

She said, "No dear, not a cellular, but a *cedula*." She gave me the definition for the word *cedula* and I began to put the cell phone back into my purse with shame.

Miko said, "See? I tried to warn you, but you wouldn't listen." Of course it had become a joke among the Dominicans; it wasn't funny at the beginning, but I laughed about it after a while.

After I had apprehended what the word *cedula* meant, I began to research it. By the time I had collected enough information to start the process, I was completely out of money. I had worked in two different Dominican companies, but they weren't paying enough. It wasn't enough to cover the rent or the bills, so I had to let it go.

A month after I was settled in Santo Domingo one of my orphanage sisters came for a visit. Miko and I, along with his brother Cucho and his girlfriend, went to pick my sister up at the bus station. When we got to the bus station, we had to wait for her to get out of customs. I had noticed she was with an older white man. When she came out of customs, I walked up to her and gave her a big hug because I had missed her. She introduced me to the stranger who was with her; she told me they had met each other on the bus. His name was Piper and he was a preacher.

Piper was supposed to meet with another preacher whose name was Micah. Micah was supposed to come pick him up at the bus station. Piper had made several attempts to call him, but he couldn't reach him. I believe the Lord had planned it this way just so I could get acquainted with Piper, because he became a great financial help to me later on in my journey. I pray that the Lord bless him more and more for everything he has done for me.

I couldn't go home that evening because I felt responsible for the man, so I invited him to come to my place. He was going to be there just for one night and he had to leave for the States the next morning. I told him in advance that I had just moved into my apartment and it was quite empty. The only piece of furniture that I had in my bedroom was one bed, the one that I had bought earlier and I had left at my friend's house. She tried to take possession of it, but that didn't work.

When I moved to my own apartment, I realized that I had need of my bed and I sent both Miko and his uncle to her house to go pick it up and bring it back to my apartment. I was kind of surprised when they had brought back my bed, because I knew if I had gone to her house myself to repossess my bed she wouldn't have given it to me. She was so determined to keep my bed, but the Lord wanted me to have it back.

Piper didn't seem to care that I hardly had anything in the house. He only needed a spot just for the night, because he had to leave the next morning. He didn't care about sleeping on the floor either. I felt the Lord wanted me to let him have my bed and I told him he could use it while my sister and I slept in the other bedroom on the floor. I remember he prayed a prayer of faith over my apartment and he said that the Lord was going to furnish the apartment in a matter of time. The Lord did hear his prayer and brought the furniture to my apartment later on. That fulfilled the scripture in the book of James 5:16, "The effectual fervent prayer of a righteous man availeth much."

We were all going through something. I remember Piper began to tell me about some of the personal issues he was having at home. He also said that he was on the verge of making a change in his life. He said the Lord told him that he was going to meet his future wife through the revival he had in Haiti, and when he met me he said that I was the one. I knew something didn't add up, because when I went to inquire of the Lord about him I felt in my spirit that he was there to help me financially. The Lord had put him in my path just to be a help to me, but I think he misunderstood the whole situation. I didn't blame him because I knew that he was going through something.

Pastor Micah finally called back, I gave him directions to my house and he showed up fifteen minutes after. I remember Piper had told his friend that he already had a place to spend the night, but he just needed a place to take a shower. My sister and I, along with Piper, got into Pastor Micah's van and he took us to his church so we could take a shower.

After we had all gotten acquainted with the pastor, and had all showered, he drove us back to my apartment and left. I introduced Miko (who was my boyfriend at the time) to Piper, but he told me that Miko wasn't the one. Because of that, Miko never did get along with Piper.

The next morning, Piper got up at 6:00 o'clock. He told me he couldn't sleep because of the rooster next door who wouldn't stop crowing every two hours. I laughed because I remember what I had to go through the very first time I moved to that neighborhood. I told him it seemed to me that this rooster was not programmed properly, and he started laughing out loud. I think he had a good laugh before he left that morning. I had

Miko call a taxi to take Piper to the airport, because he had to catch an early flight. Before he left he told me that he was going to give me a call as soon as he had arrived to his destination.

I really enjoyed my sister's visit; I took her to different places. She really enjoyed herself. There was this particular place in downtown Santo Domingo that she loved to go to. I think it's called el Conde; I also loved this place myself. There were so many beautiful sites, and people of all ethnic backgrounds. There were all kinds of restaurants and clothing stores. There were also ancient monuments, which were very fascinating; but nothing was more fascinating than the news that Piper gave me.

Man looks at the outward appearance

My sister, the guys and I went out the afternoon that Piper left. While we were in the taxi, Piper called and said that he had something to tell me. He said it was something that the Lord had shown him. I asked him, "What did the Lord show you?" and he said that I was the person that the Lord had told him about. I told him that he was probably mistaken, because I didn't feel like the Lord was leading me that way, but he told me to pray about it and see what the Lord said. I told him that I would. As much as I had prayed about it, I didn't see what he saw. I told him over and over the reason why the Lord had us meet, but he continued to be persistent about what he thought it was. My sister's visit lasted for about a week and a half, and then she left. That wasn't her last time visiting me. I encouraged her to come from time to time and she did.

I thanked the Lord for Piper because he was a constant support to me throughout my journey in Santo Domingo. He also became a close friend to me. I know he was going through so many transitions in his life at the time and I thank God that I was also a spiritual strength to him when he needed it. I pray that the Lord continues to bless him every day in his life, because he deserves it. Piper would call me every other day and we would talk about the goodness of the Lord. Other times when he called he would say, "Lina, I don't want to miss God."

I would ask him, "What do you mean by that?"

He would say, "You know — me and you."

I had to repeat myself over and over, "No, Piper. I don't think that's what the Lord meant." Of course, he was a preacher. He was probably in a higher realm in God than I was and he tried so hard to convince me, but the feeling that God had put in my heart kept getting stronger and stronger. I had to stand on what God had told me. He was a great preacher with a big heart reaching out to people and he was a big blessing to me.

I remember it was the beginning of January 2005 when I began the residency process. I had prayed and asked the Lord for the finances to get it completed, because I had no money at the time and I couldn't get a well paying job without having legal documents. The Lord gave me a miracle through someone by the name of Gutan, who became acquainted with me through a mutual friend named Jetto.

At that time, one of orphanage brothers and his friends Jetto and Morey had come to visit me and ended up staying at my apartment for three months. They came because they had an appointment with the U.S. Consulate in Santo Domingo, since the one in Haiti was temporarily closed for political reasons.

I really enjoyed their stay at my apartment, even though they broke my couch, as well as other things; it was still a joy to have them there. I remember when Jetto had introduced me to his friend Gutan through the Internet. I never thought that he would be the one that God would use to help me with my documents. Also, Jetto's girlfriend Shira was another contributor to my documents. I give thanks to the Lord because He had supplied my needs. The residency process took nearly ten months, and I didn't receive my residency card until late November 2006.

I went to apply for a job soon after I had received my Dominican ID and I got hired on the spot. I was working for a company called Wellcare as a Customer Service Representative. I was new to this field; I went through a month of training. I was so excited, and once more I felt very independent because I was providing for myself again. This job was a big blessing from the Lord, because I had prayed for a job and the Lord gave it to me.

The Bible said in Matthew 21:22, "And all things, whatsoever ye shall ask in prayer, believing, ye shall receive." Believe in God and trust him because, "He is not a man that He should lie; neither the son of man that he should repent," (Numbers 23:19). I knew the Lord had sent me to Santo Domingo for a reason and it wasn't until 2007 that I began to see it unfold.

In the process of time I met a girl named Melia whom the Lord had brought in my path. I met her through her brother, Kron. One of my orphanage brothers and his friends met Kron at the library. He wanted to know who I was and the boys introduced me to him. I got acquainted with him and he told me about his family. His mom had come to Santo Domingo to have a surgery and his sister Melia was also a student there. Kron's sister and his mom were good people and they were also Christians. Kron was the only person working in the family and he had to pay for his mom's surgery. He got released from his job after missing multiple days of work because he had to take care of his mother. There's always a reason why God sends people in your path.

Later, I found out the reason why I had met Melia. Kron's landlord wanted his apartment back, while my landlord required the same of me. In the meantime Kron had asked me to do him a favor. He wanted to know if it was all right with me to take his sister in my apartment for a little while until he could get on his feet. Of course, it was all right with me; I think Jesus would do the same. Kron brought his sister over my house for few days. I got acquainted with her and over time we became close friends. I loved her like a dear sister. Kron was no longer working and he had no place to stay. Because of that, his mom had to go back to Haiti after her surgery. Thank God the surgery went very well.

I had to move out of my apartment as well, because my landlord wanted his apartment back. Kron volunteered to help me find another apartment because he was worried about his sister. I remember he had a car, so it was easier for him to find a place for both his sister and me. A week later, Kron had found me a place. It was a two story house, and the landlord lived on the second floor. She had the first floor for rent.

Kron took me and his sister to see the house. It looked all right, but it wasn't really what I was looking for. After I checked the house, I talked to the landlord and she said she wanted three deposits in order for us to move in. I remember I had two deposits left from my previous apartment and I was lacking more money to pay for the current deposit. I spoke to Piper and I told him about it and he sent me the rest of the money that I needed. Thank you Lord, for every single time when I needed a miracle, you were always there to provide; and thank you Lord for all the people who had willing hearts to give.

I think it was in the beginning of January 2006 when we finally moved into the new apartment. I took a bedroom for myself and I let Melia use the other bedroom. Her brother stayed with her for a couple of weeks because he had nowhere to go. A month later, he found a job and a room somewhere and he moved out. I had made an agreement with him before we all moved into my apartment. The agreement was this: we both had to pay half of the rent to complete the whole monthly amount. It had become an issue on Melia's part because her brother had refused to pay for the other half of the rent. Melia wasn't working and her brother was responsible for her. I think he only paid for her rent twice and he stopped. Melia had to find a way to pay her rent. I felt bad because I couldn't afford to pay for her rent either. I did the best I could; I paid the three deposits so everyone could have a place to stay.

Melia and I had become prayer partners. We prayed every day, and the Lord began to open doors for Melia and for me as well. Melia no longer had to struggle to pay her rent. We had seen the Lord move time after time, every time we called upon His name.

There was a pastor and his wife who lived not too far away from our apartment. We got acquainted with him and he took us to his church and we enjoyed it. The pastor and his wife invited us to their home and they would feed us from time to time. They also had a son named Fred who lived with them. He was the church pianist and he also played the drums. They were good people; the pastor came to our apartment every Wednesday to conduct a Bible study.

The pastor also told us about his son; how he was single and had been looking for a wife. He said he would have loved it if it would be one of us. I believe his son at the time wasn't serious; he was jumping from one relationship to another. He wasn't the one for me, although it seemed like he was.

I remember there were times we would go without food, but we would still praise the Lord no matter the circumstances. I knew that it was my trial that I had to go through. Another problem we had at that particular house was that there was no running water and we would always have to carry water in a bucket in order to fill the tank inside the house. Almost all the places that I've rented in Santo Domingo had the same issue — no running water. I lived in that apartment for almost a year and then we moved out again.

This time, we were lacking more money to rent the next apartment. I only had one deposit left and we needed two more. We began to pray, as was our custom, and the Lord provided a Good Samaritan from that place and he completed the rest of the deposit for us.

This next apartment we moved into was more comfortable to live in, I guess because it was new. It was very spacious and it had two bedrooms, one bathroom, a kitchen, and a living room. I really liked that apartment. It was out in the country.

Melia and I moved in late November of 2007 and we found a good church home. I grew in the Lord so rapidly after I started going to that particular church. The presence of God was awesome in that place and the pastor was a very dedicated female pastor, full of the Holy Ghost.

Every Sunday when we went to church, the Lord would always have a word for us. I felt so special in the sight of the Lord. God is so real, and when you seek him in the spirit you will find him (Jeremiah 29:13). God is our refuge and strength, a very present help in trouble (Psalm 46:1).

I remember when I began to develop some issues with Melia. Her mom and sister would come and stay in our apartment as they pleased. I didn't have any problem with them visiting, but the whole issue was that the family argued almost every day. I'm a fan of peace and I'm going to keep my peace, the very peace that the Lord has left and given unto me (John 14:27).

Sometimes I would try to calm them down, but I couldn't get anywhere and I would keep my peace most of the time, then they would start all over again. Other times when the argument would heat up I would go into my bedroom and shut the door behind me until they became exhausted from screaming and yelling at each other and then they would stop. Then I would come out of my room and feel the silence and the peace and say, "Can you see how peaceful and quiet it is?" They would ignore me because they would still be mad at each other.

The Bible said that the enemy comes to steal, kill, and destroy (John 10:10). The enemy doesn't come to steal our material stuff only, but he also comes to steal and to stop all the spiritual blessings which the Lord God has for us. The Bible also says in Ephesians 4:27, "Do not give any place to the devil." We should always submit ourselves unto God; resist the enemy and he will flee from you (James 4:7). Melia's mother was also as big help to me as I was to them. When we would run out of food in our apartment, she would bring us food from Haiti. She did it out of the goodness of her heart.

Melia was a prayer warrior; she loved spending time with the Lord. She had a heart for God and that's why my spirit was connected to her spirit. It made me sad sometimes when I used to see Melia's family come and stay with her for a while, leaving me to feel lonely. However, this feeling would leave me very quickly while the spirit of the Lord would come and fill that void inside of me. I remember when her family left, she would be so sad. I didn't blame her, because she was very attached to her mom.

My roommate and I would have little misunderstandings here and there, but nothing like the arguments the family would have. Unfortunately, Melia and I couldn't live as roommates any longer; she had found a different place and waited for the right time to move out. I think sometimes we let anger get the best of us and then we lose our tempers. I do know one thing: I don't let anger rule me. We are to control our anger because the Lord gave us the spirit of self-control (2 Timothy 1:7). The Bible says that you can get angry, but don't sin (Ephesians 4:26).

The time had come for me and my roommate to separate from each other. Her mother had found her a room not too far from my apartment. We still remained close friends. I could say that when she left it wasn't the same. It was very quiet in my apartment and it didn't help the matter that I'm a quiet person, but I wasn't too disturbed by it because I had learned to manage on my own.

I was looking for a job at the time and I didn't really have the time to dwell on my loneliness. Melia would come and visit me from time to time and I would go visit her every other weekend. I remember in the process of time I was praying for a husband, because I was feeling lonely. I asked the Lord about my future husband constantly. The Lord gave me a vision in the night and told me to read Matthew 18:19 which said, "Again I say unto you, that if two of you shall agree on earth as touching anything that they shall ask, it shall be done for them of my Father which is in heaven." I thank the Lord for answering my prayer because I knew exactly what I had to do.

I couldn't wait for Melia to show up so I could give her the good news. When I told her about the scripture that the Lord had given me, she was so delighted. I told her, "Let's begin to do what the scripture said." We put our hands together in agreement and we began to declare the words of the scripture and we thanked God in the name of his son, Jesus.

After a few weeks had passed, Melia met somebody through an older gentleman that we had met at the bus station, but she never told me about it. Why was she hiding it from me? Only God knows why. She was a very secretive person. The only time I knew about anything happening in her life was if the Lord would show me; she would be very shocked and say, "That is exactly what's going on." She would be very interested to hear about what the Lord would show me.

I didn't force her to tell me about her personal life; since the time she left my apartment, the Holy Ghost would show me everything. She was very amazed. Melia was also very gifted in the area of visions and dreams. Sometimes she would also have messages from the Lord for me. While Melia had met somebody, the Lord gave me a good job. I guess it wasn't my time to be with someone yet, because the Lord still had many things to accomplish in me. That didn't stop my continuance in asking about my future husband.

Work was good; I enjoyed waking up early everyday to go to work. It was something new; I really enjoyed what I did. It was customer service where I had to answer a number of calls every day. I was exhausted and frustrated at times, especially when I had to deal with an angry customer over the phone, but other than that it felt so good to assist all kinds of people with all kinds of issues over the phone.

At my job I tried to be a light to everybody, because I was working in a place where there were all kinds of drug dealers. There were also a number of Dominicans who had been deported from the States for all kinds of criminal situations, but I knew that God still loved them and I had to do the same. In Matthew 5:16, Jesus said, "Let your light so shine before men, that they may see your good works, and glorify your Father which is in heaven."

We believers are to be a light in a world full of darkness where the truth hasn't yet been revealed (Matthew 5:14). We are to be an example and show love to everybody, whether sinners or believers, because God loves us all and he requires us to keep his commandments, especially the two greatest commandments of his law: the first is to "Love the Lord thy God with all thy heart, and with all thy soul, and with thy entire mind," (Matthew 22:37). The second is like unto it, "Thou shalt love thy neighbor as thyself," (Matthew 22:39). The scripture continues on into verse 40 and states, "On these two commandments hang all the law and the prophets."

It is not to say that you can shun the rest of the Ten Commandments, because if you love God and your neighbor you won't steal, kill, or disobey your parents, and so on. Love works no ill to his neighbor; therefore love is the fulfilling of the law (Romans 13:10). When you love God and your neighbor you will do the right thing. Jesus said, "If you do these two commandments ye shall do well."

I remember when Melia came to spend the night at my apartment one night, and I noticed that night she had been on the phone for a long time. I remember asking her as soon as she got off the phone who she was talking to and she responded and said, "Just somebody; not very important." I know she didn't want me to know, but look what the Lord did; it was unbelievable.

My roommate had developed a relationship over the phone with a guy who was soon to be her future husband. The Bible says everything that is hid shall be revealed. The moment of truth had come; on one end Melia was praying in secret to find out if this guy was the one for her, while on the other end I was still praying about my future husband and I was asking the Lord for a sign. We both prayed the same prayer that night and neither of us was aware of it. The next day before I got up, I saw in a clear vision that there was an engagement party taking place for Melia. I could hear the voice of the Lord speaking in the vision and he was telling Melia that she had been waiting for a long time and that it was her time to shine. I was kind of confused, because I knew that she didn't have a boyfriend, but at the same time I was happy for her.

I couldn't wait to call her and give her the good news. I remember when I called and I began to tell her about the vision, there was complete silence on her end. I thought something had happened and the call was dropped, but she was still there and was very shocked.

She said to me, "Oh Lina, you didn't even know. I didn't tell you anything about it because I didn't think it was going to work, but I was praying and asking the Lord to give me a sign that night. I never did receive anything from the Lord, but instead He gave you an answer for me." I knew she was trying to hide this whole thing from me, but the Lord revealed the matter to me early that morning. She didn't know what to think, but I knew she was very pleased and very happy that the Lord had answered her prayer.

In the meantime, I was still working. Not only was I so happy for Melia, but I was also humbled that the Lord was using me in a special way. In the process of time I had met a young woman through a Dominican friend of mine. This young woman's name was Netta. Netta told me her story and it was very touching. She couldn't find any decent place to stay since she had moved to Santo Domingo.

She told me that she was robbed multiple times. Furthermore, she said that a couple of thieves had broken into her place and stolen her money and other things as well. I told her that she could rent the other room in my apartment; she was so relieved. I remember telling her that I was going to move out of that apartment very soon. She said that was fine with her and that she would be looking for another place once the time came.

I knew a man who had a vehicle. He heard about Netta and offered to help her, so Netta and I got into his car and we went to her old place to help her move all of her stuff into my apartment. Netta seemed like a nice person, but she wasn't a Christian.

I was so determined to help her out in any way that I could, but it didn't work. I told her about my church and she said that she would go with me on that upcoming Sunday. On Sunday I woke up early so I could get to church on time. Netta was also up early. I thought she was getting ready for church, but I could tell by the way she was dressed that she wasn't going to church. She got out before I did, and she said that she was sorry but she couldn't make it to church that Sunday, but she hoped to make it next Sunday.

Netta was very loud; that was her nature. I remember when the neighbors began to complain about her and how she was disturbing their peace; they told me that I had to do something about it. I went to her room and I brought the neighbors' complaints to her attention.

I was kind of surprised by her answer. She didn't seem to care, nor did she listen either; I knew I was in for another battle. The Bible said in Ephesians 6:12, "For we wrestle not against flesh and blood, but against principalities, against powers, against the rulers of the darkness of this world, and against spiritual wickedness in high places." I didn't have to fight this battle; I held my peace. The Lord took care of it, because the battle belongs to Him.

I went through this battle for about two and a half months. I remember before she left my apartment she went to Haiti to visit her son and her parents. She told me that she was going to be gone for a few weeks, but ended up being gone for almost a month. She never contacted me to let me know what was going on. I thought something must have happened to her. She came on a day that I wasn't expecting her and the funny thing was that she wasn't alone.

I came home that day and to my surprise, there she was with her boyfriend in her room. After she had introduced me to her boyfriend, I told her she could have told me that she was bringing somebody with her. She said that she tried to call me, but it wasn't true. I noticed that she was trying to bring up excuses and that she wasn't going to listen to me anyway. Netta and her boyfriend argued and fought almost every day. Her boyfriend told me that he was not a mean person, but Netta caused him to be somebody else when he got mad. I remember telling him, "If you two can't get along, then it's better for both of you to separate from each other before anything serious happens."

He said, "I've tried time after time to leave her, but I couldn't do it because I loved her so much."

I looked at him and said, "Love doesn't hurt; love is kind," (1 Corinthians 13:4).

Things didn't get better with Netta, and they weren't going to. She kept getting more out of control from day to day. I reminded her about what I had told her from the beginning when she first moved to my apartment. Because she wouldn't listen and because of her rude behavior, I asked her to leave and find another place to stay. Of course she didn't like it, but there was nothing else I could do. I tried to help her in every way that I could, but it didn't work.

Netta's boyfriend finally left two weeks later, but Netta was still in the same shape. I remember praying to the Lord and asking him to take care of this situation, and the Lord did. That Sunday morning I woke up to go to church and when I got there I noticed that my pastor had invited a guest to preach the word of God that morning. As usual the presence of God was awesome in that place, as well as the praise and worship songs.

I remember when the pastor took the pulpit and delivered the message, it was powerful.

After he preached his sermon he began to tell the congregation that the Lord had a word for several of us, and that the Lord was going to move mightily. The first person he called out was me, and the spirit of the Lord began to speak out of him and he began to tell me that deliverance had come to my house that day. Furthermore, he said to me that the Lord had seen my affliction, and He had seen what I was going through and He had come to deliver me. God delivered me spiritually as well as physically that day. When I went back home, Netta was gone. The peace of God had once more reigned in my apartment.

Unfortunately, you will find people like Netta who will come across your path. They seem so harmless, but inwardly they are ravenous wolves. We believers have got to have our spiritual eyes open. If you can't see in the spirit, ask God who gives freely to all men and He will do it for you. God loves it when we ask him for spiritual things, because He knows that the natural things are not really important. He already knows that we have need of them, which is why He said for us not to worry about what we're going to eat and drink, but seek ye first the kingdom of God and his righteousness and all these other things shall be added unto you, (Matthew 6:33).

After the whole scenario with Netta was over with, I made up my mind not to have another roommate living in my apartment anymore. I thank God for being there for me, especially in times of trouble. God will take care of your enemies if you hold your peace. Jesus said in Matthew 5:44, "Love your enemies, bless them that curse you, do good to them that hate you, and pray for them which despitefully use you, and persecute you." I know it's not easy, but if we obey the word of God, you will prosper.

When we disobey, there are consequences that will follow. There are many times I found myself in very difficult situations because I didn't listen to the Lord. After Netta left I was still working, keeping the rent up to date, and taking care of other bills. I ended up moving out of that apartment not too long after Netta left. I remember right before I moved out, an incident had happened on the second floor. One night there were some robbers who had broken into the second floor.

Four people were living in that apartment — a woman and her sister, and two of her brothers — but thank God that when the thieves had broken in that night they were all asleep. They didn't find out until they woke up in the morning and found the living room empty. I thank God for sparing me that night, because I was alone in my apartment. I knew one thing for sure, that I was covered under the shadow of the Almighty (Psalm 91:1).

I had another friend named Julo who was helping me find another place to live. I was working and I didn't have enough time to go house hunting. Ever since those thieves had broken into the second floor I felt an urge in my spirit to move out of my apartment quickly; I knew it had to be God. I felt like I was being watched and my apartment was going to be the next one to be broken into.

Julo came over to my apartment one weekend afternoon and said that he had found me another place. I was so happy; I hopped on his motorcycle to go and check out the new place. It was already after dark and when we got there he spoke to the landlord and introduced me as the new tenant. She began to ask me questions, and she wanted to know if I was a Christian. I replied, "Yes, I am." I guess because I was wearing pants and earrings, in her eyes I wasn't qualified as a Christian. Jesus said, not to judge on the outward appearance, but to look on the heart (1 Samuel 16:7). It's not what you look like on the outside that determines if you are a Christian; it's what's on the inside.

I know that I'm free, praise God! I'm no longer living under the curse of the law. Jesus Christ, the Lamb of God, paid the debt; the ultimate price for you and me. If you haven't accepted Him yet as your Lord and Savior, it's never too late. While you still have your breath, accept Him in your heart today and allow Him to be the Savior and Shepherd of your soul. He came that we may have life, and have life more abundantly (John 10:10). He said if you deny Him before men He will also deny you before His Father in Heaven (Matthew 10:33).

We don't want to deny the One who has suffered and died in our place. He has shed his precious blood on the cross for us, and now because of Him salvation is free and personal. There's only one way to Heaven and it is through Jesus Christ, our Lord and Savior (John 14:6).

When I finally moved out of that apartment, it was on a rainy day. The truck driver who was moving my stuff out of the apartment didn't seem very friendly. I remembered that he had asked me if I knew the place where I was moving to and my response was, "I think so." It seemed like he had an impression that I didn't really know where I was going, and he was right. When we finally got on the road, I only knew the first turn and after that I was lost. The driver kept asking me which way to go and I kept misleading him, but I didn't do it on purpose.

After a while he stopped the truck in anger and began to ask directions from different pedestrians passing by, but still it availed nothing. Finally he spoke up out of frustration and said, "If I have to make one more wrong turn, I'm gonna take you back to your old apartment." He stopped his truck above the road that led to my new apartment. I was praying in my mind that the Lord would help me find the way, and then suddenly the Lord opened up my eyes and showed me where I was; I was so relieved. I pointed out to my right and said, "There's my new place." For the first time during the whole trip, that truck driver had a smile on his face. I guess it wasn't that bad after all.

A Friend that's closer than a brother

Later that night, I set everything in order in my new place and was ready to go back to work the next day. It took me a while to get used to the directions to my new apartment. I got acquainted with the landlord and her husband and kids. Her name was Sister Annette; she was a woman of God, a prayer warrior. She had seven kids. Sister Annette was so dedicated and sold out to God. She spent lots of time in prayer with me; we became prayer partners. She was a very good person. I remember when Sister Annette used to go days without food in her home, but she would not tell anybody. The Lord showed me her situation and from then on I became a helper to her and her family.

I remember when I would come from work, change my clothes and I walk next door to Sister Annette's house. She would be so happy to see me and converse with me. We would always talk about the Lord and all of his goodness. She invited me to her church and I went with her. I believe we walked for half an hour to get to her church, but when I got there it was very rewarding.

I didn't cook that much at home since I was alone. I used to contribute my share each day with Annette's family so that I could eat dinner with them. Sister Annette and I became very close friends and we were also connected in the spirit. I remember one night we had a prayer meeting at her place; the presence of the Lord was very strong there. We prayed for a good while and sang praise and worship songs, and then we prayed again until it was five o'clock in the morning. I was very exhausted, but it didn't really matter to me because I would do anything for my Lord.

Six weeks after I moved to my new place, it happened at my job that the project I was working on had come to an end. I was told to go home until further notice. I remember it was kind of devastating. If it hadn't been for the deposits that I had saved up, things wouldn't have looked good for me at all. I noticed how sweet and spiritual my landlord was until this incident happened, then she changed. I was praying that the Lord would bring a new project to the surface so I could go back to work and pay my rent.

I went back to my job on Monday morning, and to my amazement the secretary told me that they had a new project that would begin within the next week. She told me to get ready for a phone call and that I would start working again the following week. I was so happy and I thanked the Lord for answering my prayer.

I went two whole months without a job and it wasn't easy. Piper had been supporting me still, but I didn't want to rely on him too much.

When I started working again, my landlord brought it to my attention that I couldn't rent her place without a deposit because it was against the law. I told her that I would take care of it. In the process of time I remember I was looking for another place, because there was no running water in the house and because I had lived out the deposits while I had not been working. She had suggested that it would be better for me if I found another place. I told her, "Since I'm fixing to move out of your place then I don't need to build up the deposits that I've used," but I had paid my rent every month.

The Bible says in Luke 18:1 that men should always pray, and not to faint. I did a three day fast; it wasn't three full days, but I fasted from 8 o'clock to noon each day. On the third day of my fast, one of the neighbors came knocking at my door and said that he had found me another apartment. I thanked the Lord that he had accepted the sacrifice that I made and provided another place for me. My neighbor took me to check out the new place and when I came to it I loved what I saw.

I had two options at the time, but the first apartment that I looked into was isolated from neighbors, and since I was alone I didn't think it was a good idea for me to move there. The second apartment was the one that I was looking for; it was a unit. I noticed that it was surrounded by other apartments and I wasn't alone. I spoke to the landlord and he asked for four deposits. I remember asking him if there was any running water in his apartment and he said yes, but I told him I wasn't going to pay four deposits; it wasn't right.

I had never heard of four deposits before and I said to him maybe it would be better if I rented the first apartment; at least I didn't have to pay four deposits. He looked at me and said, "How much do you have?"

I replied, "Three deposits, as usual."

He said, "Let's do it." I was kind of surprised when I found out later that this man was a pastor.

I went back home and told Sister Annette about the new apartment and I mentioned to her that I was very excited about it. I remember she said that she was praying that the Lord would send somebody just like me to rent her place. Unfortunately, when I moved out of her apartment the family that had moved in was not what she had expected.

The area that I had moved into had at least ten small units and there were other apartments in the area. I lived in unit one. I got acquainted with three different neighbors who were very good people. I ministered the gospel to couple of them and they really enjoyed it. I didn't really spend too much time in my neighborhood because I didn't really know anybody there.

I spent most of my time with Sister Annette after I had got off of work each day. I remember telling Sister Annette to help me pray for a husband because I was alone, and she said that God would give me a good husband. I came to a point where I was getting very desperate and I said to the Lord, "If you don't give me somebody then I will tie the knot with the next person that comes in my path."

Then the Lord began to show me about certain people in visions and dreams. There were couple of guys that I had seen in my visions at different times and I knew that they weren't the one. The first one came and told me that the Lord sent him, but I replied to him that I knew he was coming and also that he wasn't the one. He was kind of surprised and said, "How do you know that I'm not the one?"

I replied again and said to him, "The Lord showed me about you two weeks before you came." At that moment he didn't know what else to say. Jesus said for us to watch, because there are many false prophets in this world that have gone out before us. There are many people who don't believe that God speaks, but I know that the Lord speaks to me most of the time through visions and dreams. I can also hear His voice in the clear of the day, especially when I begin to read His word, and when I pray as well.

Back in the old times, He spoke to his servants the prophets in like manner. Some he spoke mouth to mouth, like with Moses, Samuel, and tons of others. It is as simple as this; if you have a relationship with the Lord, you will hear His voice. He said in Proverbs 3:5-6, "Trust in the Lord with all your heart and lean not on your on understanding; in all your ways acknowledge him, and he shall direct thy path." Let the Lord guide you in every major decision and any drastic move that you're about to make, and believe me, you'll not regret it. He has guided me until now and He will guide me every step of the way. Dear readers, God never makes mistakes; all you have to do is trust Him.

I remember not too long after that, I met the second guy that I had seen previously in my vision. He was this new employee in my job and for some reason almost all the women were falling for him. He and I were sitting in the same row; actually he was sitting next to me. I got acquainted with him and I found out that he fathered seven kids with seven different women, but still that didn't stop him because he thought that I would fall for him too. I could've fallen for him, don't get me wrong, because he was good to look upon, but I thank God that He had stopped me from making this terrible mistake. The Bible says that Satan comes as an angel of light to deceive many (2 Corinthians 11:14).

Jesus said for us to watch and pray so we don't fall into temptation (Mark 14:38). "All that there is in the world, the lust of the flesh, the lust of the eyes, and the pride of life." It doesn't come from the Father, but from the world (1 John 2:16). If we remember His law and keep it, then we will not have to worry about making any mistakes.

MY FIRST VISITATION

In the beginning of the year 2009, I had a visitation from the Lord, but prior to that visitation the Lord spoke to me and told me that my landlord had robbed me. I remember it was on a Saturday morning while I was cleaning my apartment that the Lord spoke these words in my ear. I waited until my landlord walked by my apartment and I called him. I asked him if I could exchange a few words with him and he replied yes. I didn't tell him that the Lord had spoken to me, but I acted upon the word of the Lord and said, "The money that you took from me; what was it for?"

Then he said, "You know. I had already told you." I reminded him about his words; he said it was to install the electricity in my apartment, but it was for something else. He began to stutter over his words; the Lord was right about him. He then went on to say, "We'll talk about it later and you'll get your money back," but I knew that wasn't going to happen. I told him that he needed to make things right between us, but he got mad and said that ever since I moved into his apartment I had been a problem. I think he didn't like it because the Lord had revealed who he really was.

My landlord lied about having running water in the apartment and he also lied about installing the power in my apartment. The other tenants must have been afraid of him; they were having all kinds of issues in their apartments but wouldn't tell him about it. Lastly, he belittled me by saying that he didn't converse with his tenants.

What a good thing it is when you can hear what the Lord is saying and He reveals the tricks of the enemy. I was so hurt and I went back to my house weeping before the Lord. I said to the Lord, "Why did this man speak to me like I was nothing? Is it because I don't own a piece of property, or because I don't own a home?" But I know the God that I serve owns it all. He owns cattle upon a thousand hills (Psalm 50:10). He can bless me at any given time, but our job as Christians is to search the kingdom of God first and His righteousness and all the other things shall be added unto us (Matthew 6:33).

I love this scripture in the Bible where it talks about how weeping may endure for a night, but joy cometh in the morning (Psalm 30:5). That's what happened to me the next day, which (ironically) was a Sunday morning. I remember that I woke up to get ready for church and as I was sitting on the side of my bed meditating, suddenly I wasn't in my bedroom anymore, I was translated into another place. I found myself riding in a big crowded bus which was taking us to Wal-Mart. When we got there I waited for everyone to get off the bus. There was a waiting line where people were getting food and drinks; I stood there inside the bus watching.

After everyone had gotten off the bus, I then got off. I remember my ex-roommate was there too, and I was telling her about a vision I had about her. As I was speaking to her I could see there was something shiny that was capturing the corner of my eye, and when I looked up in the sky I was amazed by what I saw. I said to my roommate, "Look at the sun." I said to her again, "I have never seen the sun shining so bright. Could this be the sun?"

Lo and behold, it wasn't the sun. It was that big bright Light, the Lord Jesus Christ, in all His glory. It was very awesome. As I kept gazing at the Light, it came down from the sky and it passed on before me. It came very close to me as it went by. When I looked up, every single one of the people who were there in that place had fled. They all went inside the mall because they were afraid.

My roommate and I were the only ones who were left outside. I remember I spoke up and said, "Strange things are happening in this place." As we continued on our conversation, the whole place where I was standing was covered with clouds — bright white clouds. That's when I decided it was time for me to go inside, because I didn't understand at that time what was happening in the spirit.

I remember when God appeared to Moses in the burning bush, he told Moses to take off his sandals for the place he was standing on was holy ground. That is the reason why there wasn't anybody standing in that place, because none of us was worthy to stand in His presence. As I stood in front of that glass door, I was contemplating the glory of God in that place when all of a sudden I saw two white hands coming out of the clouds, reaching out towards me. I, in turn, reached out and touched His hand, but before He could even speak to me, I heard Him in my heart as if He was saying to me, "I love you."

Immediately it sounded like an intercom opened and I heard Him in a loud, clear voice saying to me, "I love you." Furthermore, He said to me, "Go tell my people that I love them and I'm waiting for them with my arms wide open." God wants us to repent from our wicked ways and come back to Him (2 Chronicles 7:14).

When I came back to myself and was back in my bedroom again, I kept wondering what had just happened. Then, as I was pondering to myself, I heard a dog crying out behind my window. I got off my bed and I went to my window to see what was wrong with that dog, but there was nothing wrong with the dog; amazingly, that dog felt the presence of God around the house. I was speechless. I couldn't understand what was happening, but I knew it was all good. Thank you, Jesus!

Sometimes I say to myself that I'm not worthy of Him to share his glory with me, but it was always my heart's desire to see Jesus. I thank the Lord for allowing me to see His glory.

After I finally got ready for church, I decided to take a taxi. As I was coming up the road, my roommate didn't recognize me. It wasn't until I came closer to the church that she recognized who I was. As I approached her I asked her, "What do you see?" She wouldn't tell me. She said for some reason I looked strange, but I didn't tell her what happened to me that morning. I figured it wasn't time for me to say anything yet. The Lord had filled my heart with so much joy because of that visitation. That visitation to me is worth more than anything anyone could ever possess in this world. It is an unforgettable treasure that will stay with me for the rest of my life.

I remember for a week after the Lord had visited me, I couldn't let my arm down because of the weight of the glory of God where He had touched my hand. Since then, the presence of the Lord and the cloud and the light had not left me. Wherever I am, I can feel His presence and I can see His bright Light from time to time. Jesus said He'll never leave us nor forsake us, but He will be with us always even unto the very end (Hebrews 13:5).

The Lord told me that whenever I testify about my encounter with Him to the world, if people will believe it, they will be healed immediately of whatsoever disease they have. Do you believe it? With God, it is a trust issue. He said that without faith it is impossible to please Him (Hebrews 11:6). We need to believe in God and believe that He can do all things. When you believe, things begin to happen, and when you doubt you do without, but God still remains faithful to His word.

BEING LED BY THE HOLY SPIRIT

It was in the middle of 2009 when the Lord began to speak to me through visions and dreams. He began to give me instructions of what I had to do. I remember it was on an early Saturday morning when I had this clear vision from the Lord. He said to me, "Remember the application you were filling out for Canada? I want you to complete it, because I'm sending you to the consulate, whose name is Lewis." The Lord told me that He had already spoken to the consulate about me concerning a tourist visa.

I was so amazed, but then again I began to doubt. I said "Lord, you know I don't have enough money to apply for a visa," but He never mentioned anything about money. I just brushed the vision off my spirit as if to say to the Lord, "Thank you for the good news, Lord, but I'm not interested."

Melia had spent the night at my house and when we woke up in the morning, I told her about the vision and what the Lord had told me to do. She was excited and said, "Do whatever He said." I told her that I couldn't afford to take that route.

One week later, about the same day at the same time, another vision came to me.

It was the Lord again, and He said to me, "Girl, I told you that I've got good news for you. I have opened a door for you wherever you'd like to go, either Canada or the States. You choose, because the door is open." I woke up again that morning with tears of joy and I could hear the Lord speaking to my heart saying, "I will always take care of you."

The Lord Jesus said in His word to cast our burdens unto Him, because He cares for us (Psalm 55:22). He doesn't want us to worry about anything. This time, I began to take my visions seriously. I told the Lord that I didn't have enough money, but the Lord had never mentioned anything about finances. I was getting too anxious about things that didn't really matter to the Lord. I told Sister Annette about the visions that I had been having and all the things that the Lord had spoken to me. She was very happy. At work, I was so excited about the Lord and how He was speaking to me that I began to share my experiences with some of my co-workers.

For a couple of weeks I noticed that the Lord wasn't speaking and I was concerned with what the reason might have been. One Saturday morning, Sister Annette came to my house to pray with me and after we prayed she told me that the Lord said I was talking too much. Also, I was sharing too much about the assignment that I was told to do. I admitted to it, because I really did share too much. Sometimes when God speaks to you and He wants you to do something it is for you, not for your neighbors or your friends, only for you.

People may lead you in the wrong direction. You know the voice of God; you go and do what He says to do. You don't need any man's approval when God tells you to do something. At the end of the day when the task remains undone, you're the one that will give an account to God, because you were the only one who heard His voice. I repented to the Lord and I confessed to never say a word unless He wanted me to.

I wasn't really working on the Lord's assignment, because in my mind I thought it was impossible, but the Lord wouldn't leave me alone until I completed that assignment. He kept on showing me visions and dreams about the visa; He even showed me things about the airport and the airplane. The Lord even gave me a vision that I was in Florida visiting my missionary folks, but I didn't tarry too long. I told them that I must leave and Mr. Singleton spoke up and said that he would walk me to the door.

After he walked me to the door, as soon as I stepped outside, there were dead bodies everywhere as far as your eyes could see. I was in shock; I couldn't tell what had happened. I didn't hear any sound whatsoever; I was the only living person walking among the dead. I felt so bad for these people, and I was kind of afraid as I was walking out of that place. When I woke up, I thought about the vision and I said, "Lord have mercy, because whatever it is, it's going to be terrible."

There was this guy that I knew back when I was a teenager who had tried to start a relationship with me in the past, but it didn't work because I was too young and very immature. Ten years later, he started calling me on the phone. He told me that he had just gone through a divorce and I expressed my sympathy to him. He told me how mean and deceitful his wife was, but I thank God that I was able to speak peace in his life. I was able to help him spiritually and mentally. There was no time for courtship — he needed help and the Lord was there to meet his needs.

I remember the Lord told me not to take anything from him, and I knew why. In the meantime I asked the Lord if he was the one, but I never got an answer.

He kept on calling every other day. I guess it was to release the hurt, the wound, and the betrayal of his estranged wife. There was nothing I could do, but I tried to be a spiritual support to him. I remember one time we were talking over the phone and he asked me if I was coming to the States. I told him that the Lord had already told me to go get a visa. I told him that I didn't know what to do because of finance-related issues. He said, "Well, how much do you need?" I remembered what the Lord had told me and I quickly replied that it wasn't necessary. My cell phone at the time was broken and I couldn't get good reception from it. He offered to send me a brand new cell phone and again I had to turn his offer down. It was nothing against him — he was a very nice person and he was very humble.

The reason why the Lord didn't want me to accept anything from his hands was because he wasn't my future husband, which I found out a month later when the Lord revealed it to me in a vision. The Lord told me that I was going to be with a white guy. I thanked the Lord for the clarification.

I remember that I went to the secretary at my job and I told her that I needed a letter of recommendation and she told me to stop by within three days to get it. In the meantime I went to the bank and requested a bank statement, and got it on the spot. I called Mr. Singleton and I told him that I needed a letter of invitation and he sent it through the mail. One thing that I do know is that the Lord never mentioned anything about letters or documents, but only the application. I knew that I wasn't paying enough attention.

The day finally arrived for my interview at the consulate. It was the 17th of December 2009, and my appointment was at 7:30 am. I had set my alarm clock for 5 am and made some arrangements with the taxi driver because he was one of my neighbors. It must have been the Lord who woke me up that morning, because the alarm clock didn't go off. When I looked at the clock it was almost 6:00. I know how long it takes me to get ready, but thank God that morning it took me less than an hour.

When I went outside, the taxi driver was gone and I thought, "Oh Lord, I blew my appointment." I decided to go knock on his door and I could hear his wife from the inside asking who it was. I told her that it was me and she said, "My child, what are you doing outside at this time?" It was still dark. I told her that I had an appointment with her husband. She said, "You can't trust this man." She then went on and said, "I wished you could have talked to me instead of him." I told her that I didn't know her husband too well. It was a trick of the devil, trying to hinder God's purpose for my life, but the devil is a liar and the father of lies (John 8:44).

She came out and said that she would help me get a taxi. She said that it wasn't safe for me to be outside alone at this time. My neighbor knew of a man nearby who was a taxi driver so we walked to his house, but his wife said that he had already left. I was getting worried because the time was passing by, but I asked the Lord to provide a taxi for me. While I tarried, talking to the taxi-driver's wife, a taxi came driving slowly down the road. We stopped the taxi and my neighbor asked him to prove himself. He showed us his taxi's tag, and she looked at me and said, "It's all right; now you can go with him."

While in the taxi, the driver asked about my destination and I told him to take me to the U.S. consulate. We got there just in time; thank God! I was able to position myself in the waiting line outside, but it took a long while for my interview to begin. When I finally got inside the building, I had to wait again for about a couple of hours. There were so many people waiting to be attended to at the same time, it was unreal.

Finally, I heard my name called through the intercom with several other names; it was finally my turn. As I stood before the consulate, he began to interrogate me concerning my application. I remember the first question he asked me was, "Where do you work?" In response to his question, I opened up my folder to take out my recommendation letter and he stopped me and said, "No, I need to hear it from your mouth." So I told him where my job was located. The second question he asked me was, "How much do you make?" Again, I opened up my folder to take out the bank statement, but he stopped me again and said, "Did I ask you to see any kind of papers?" He then added, "I don't believe in papers. I want to hear the answer come from your mouth." So I told him how much I made and he said it wasn't enough.

The third question he asked me was, "Where are you going?" This time I didn't bother to open up my folder anymore; I told him directly where I was going. When I began to think back concerning the instructions that the Lord had given me about the application, He never mentioned any other papers except the application. No wonder the consulate had refused to see any of my letters, because the word of the Lord had come to pass.

After the interview was over, the consulate said that he would grant me a three month visa because of one thing — because he could see where I had been in the States before, but had returned. Little did he know that it was part of God's plan. I was so happy to see how the Lord had performed His word which He spoke to me about a month before my interview. I praised the Lord for His faithfulness. "God is not a man that he should lie; neither the son of man, that he should repent," (Numbers 23:19). You can bet your all on God; He will never lie to you.

The joy that the Lord had filled my heart with was beyond words. I went to Sister Annette's house and surprised her with the good news. She was very happy to see how real the Lord was in my life. I remember she told me of a night vision she had about me. She said she saw me leaving Santo Domingo and I was selling all of my belongings. I knew that the Lord had a plan, but I didn't know the extent of it. I began to witness God's plan unfolding little by little before my very eyes.

I remember right before I left Santo Domingo, I had a second encounter with that bright light. I remember it was 2 am when the Holy Spirit woke me up to pray. After I was through praying, I had lain back on my bed, but had not yet fallen asleep. All of a sudden, the Lord translated my spirit to my work place. There were at least 16 people on the floor taking calls. While I sat on my seat taking calls, a high volume of calls flooded through my phone line. I got up to tell my supervisor about it, when all at once I began to see people running within the building to find a place where they could hide. Even the security guard ran for his life; there was something invisible coming through that door. Whatever it was, I knew it was evil.

I was the only one left standing inside the building and I thought within myself that I needed to find a place to hide as well. Every door that I tried to open was locked, but finally I found an open door and quickly ran inside of it. Before me was a little window with the blind over it; I remember telling the Lord, "Whatever it is, don't let it find me."

Do you know that 2 Timothy 1:7 says that God did not give us the spirit of fear; but of power and of love, and of a sound mind? He said don't be afraid of the terror by night, nor of the arrow that flies by day (Psalm 91:5). Jesus also said He gave us authority over all the powers of the enemy (Luke 10:19). We have power over sickness and diseases and when we speak his word, they've got to leave in Jesus' name.

When my spirit was finally back in my bedroom again, I noticed that my room was a mess. My fan was on when there was no electricity, and my two Bibles were on my bed. Usually I kept my Bibles on the shelf, but for some reason they were both on my bed and the air was blowing through the pages. My laptop, however, was opened and there was this particular song playing from it which said, "You must worship me!"

I remember I couldn't stand to hear this song and I tried to bury my laptop underneath my pillow. It was like all hell had broken loose in my room, but all of a sudden I saw the light appear through my bedroom door. It was that same bright light that I had seen during my first encounter with the Lord. It was more beautiful and brighter than the sun, and all at once everything had ceased, because Jesus was in the house.

About two weeks after I had my second encounter with that bright Light, a drastic change began to take place at my job. A lot of people had been laid off because the Wellcare staff had decided not to renew their contract that year with the Dominican company for which I worked. Every week they would send at least 10 people home, until there were 15 of us left. Imagine the volume of calls that were coming through our phone lines; it was double the work. Here again, that open vision the Lord gave me had come to pass. I remember that I told my supervisor that I was going to be away for Christmas vacation and He gave me leave for three weeks.

Before the Lord sent me to the States, He gave me a scripture: Matthew 10:10. The scripture said, "Nor scrip for your journey, neither two coats, neither shoes, nor yet staves: for the workman is worthy of his meat." At that particular time I didn't really understand the exact meaning of this verse, because I was very young in the Lord, but three months later I got married to my wonderful husband, and immediately after that we began to go through all kinds of trials and tribulation together. I then found out what that scripture really meant.

Reunited

I didn't really want to travel alone, so I contacted my missionary folks to make some arrangements with them. They said that they were going to be in Haiti on the 27th of December 2009, but they would leave Haiti on the 2nd of January 2010. I told them that I'd be there. I packed my suitcases that night and left Santo Domingo the next day to go to Haiti. When I arrived at the Dominican border it was very crowded and I got robbed by some so-called Dominican guards, along with some Haitians who were supposed to be their associates. I was also robbed by the Haitian motorcycle rider who took me to the Haitian border. Thank God I had some type of money on me that they couldn't see (which didn't belong to me), and the Lord gave me wisdom where to hide it.

It was a long day and I was very exhausted. My orphanage sister was supposed to pick me up at the bus station, but when I got there she was nowhere to be found. I had to borrow the driver's cell phone in order to communicate with her — my phone was disabled because I was in a different country. I told her where I was and we finally found each other; what a relief it was. I told her what happened to me at the border and she couldn't stop laughing. It's interesting how she thought it was funny, but by the end of the day I was laughing too.

I spent that night at my sister's house and in the following morning we both went up to the mountains to the orphanage to be reunited with the Singletons and the other orphanage kids. I was so thrilled to see everybody again, because it had been a long time since I had last seen them. We had devotions that night like we always had in the past, and the presence of the Lord was there. It was so good to see everybody again.

The next day, which was the 30th of December that same year, I got to spend some more time with the Singletons; I really enjoyed it. I told Mr. Singleton that I would need some help getting my plane ticket because of the robbery that took place at the Dominican border while I was coming out. He said, "Not a problem." The next day we both went to the travel agency to buy our plane tickets. The Singletons and I were all set to leave on the 2nd of January 2010.

I remember I told my sister that I had to be at a church meeting for the new year, so we both went down to the city and attended the church service until midnight while we were entering into the New Year 2010. I met with an old friend after the service that night and I asked her if it was possible to speak with my former principal, but she told me that the principal wasn't in Haiti at the time. She gave me her phone number and told me that the principal was in Florida.

I told her that I was going to leave for the States in a few days, and that I would contact her by phone when I arrived. I then told her about the Lord's assignment and the reason why I had to get in touch with the principal.

I couldn't go back up to the mountains that early morning, so my sister and I spent the night at Vicki's house (another orphanage sister). I woke up early that morning and told my sister that I had to get to the orphanage as soon as possible because the Singletons and I had to catch an early flight the next day. Thank God, I got there just in time to make my suitcase.

The next day, which was the 2nd of January 2010, the Singletons and I flew to Florida and when we got to their place we were so tired. It was so cold that it hurt. I don't think I've ever been so cold in my life, but the inside of their home was a cozy and comfortable place. I was surprised to see Angel (their dog) again, but she wasn't alone — she had a family. I remembered her since puppyhood; she was very small. I think Angel is even blessed to have the Singletons as part of her family.

I also saw the Singleton's children again, Ferra and Troy, who were all grown up. Ferra had a baby girl whose name was Connie; I think she's now 4 years old. I enjoyed her so much; I got to babysit her a couple of times. She was the cutest thing I had ever seen. Troy, however, was now a mature, responsible young man; he is now married to his lovely wife Ann.

One night, the Singletons had to go to the hospital to visit a missionary friend who was very sick, and they told me that they weren't going to tarry and they would be back in an hour. Something happened to their male dog while they were gone and it startled me so much. Ody Joe, the male dog, had a seizure and I didn't know what in the world to do so I panicked because I thought he was going to die. As I calmed myself down and I took a deep breath, I was thinking about what to do in this situation. It came to my spirit to pray for him, so I laid my hand upon his head and I began to rebuke the seizure, and thank God, he went back to normal and the seizure left him.

When the Singletons returned, I told them what had happened to Ody Joe and Mrs. Singleton responded, "Oh that happens to him from time to time." I just wished they could've said something before they left the house. At least it wouldn't have scared me that bad.

Mr. Singleton is a very busy man; he is now the executive director of a missionary training school. They couldn't have chosen a better candidate to do this job. He is doing an excellent job and if you're considering becoming a missionary, you are to contact him via Facebook for more information. They've got the best teaching and training, and you won't regret it.

Mrs. Singleton is a school teacher, and she too is doing an awesome job teaching the kindergarteners. Dear readers, these are the two awesome people who gave their life up, left everything behind, and came to raise me as an orphan in the way of the Lord. Not only me, but eighteen other kids as well; to God be the glory. I'm so grateful to the Lord and also grateful for the fact that they obeyed the Lord and came to fulfill this ministry. They did an outstanding job and I know that God is well pleased with them.

Now we all have become grown men and women of God, all because they stepped up to the plate. Almost all of us are married with kids; what a great blessing from the Almighty God. I believe that the Lord is looking for more people like Mr. and Mrs. Singleton who will not stagger at His voice or His word. We are to make ourselves available to the Lord all the time. I believe there is a greater blessing awaiting them not only in Heaven, but also in the appointed time on Earth as well.

I stayed over at the Singleton's for about three weeks. I really enjoyed the time we spent together. I went several times to help Mrs. Singleton in her class. It was so much fun; it brought back memories of the times when I used to teach kindergarten back in the year 2000.

I remember something terrible happened while I was in Florida. A 7.0 magnitude earthquake hit my country on the 12th of January 2010, ten days after I left Haiti. Another great miracle that the Lord had done for me; He saved my life. Thank you, Jesus! The vision I saw concerning the dead bodies everywhere in that particular place had come to pass right before my eyes. I remembered I was the only living person walking among the dead and look where I was — in Florida, out of harm's way. Praise the Almighty God for the good things He has done.

A new plan

After the tragedy, the loss, and the terrible chaos that the earthquake had left behind in Haiti, President Obama granted an 18-month visa to all of the Haitian nationals who were in the States at the time of the earthquake. I went online and read about the President's declaration and I told the Singletons that I would go for it. Mr. Singleton told me about Terrence, Mrs. Singleton's brother-in-law, who was a lawyer. Mr. Singleton said he would be the perfect one to help me with this case. He contacted Terrence by phone and told him about me and about my situation, and Terrence said that he would help me.

Janelle, the oldest girl in the orphanage, had sent her three kids to the States for reason of the earthquake, and they were all staying at the Singleton's house as well. The Singletons had a full house with me and Janelle's three kids being there. They didn't have enough room for all of us, so Mrs. Singleton's sister Bonnie and her husband Terrence had volunteered to take Janelle's kids into their home for a while, because they had a bigger house.

Mrs. Singleton asked me if I wanted to go to Indiana to help Bonnie out with Janelle's three kids, because Bonnie had three kids of her own. I knew I had to be in Indiana because Terrence was working on my TPS documents. Terrence and Bonnie were also a great couple with very good hearts. I know they didn't have to do what they did, but they did it out of the goodness of their hearts. They treated Janelle's kids like they were their own. They signed them up for the same school that their own kids were attending; I know that they spoiled these kids. They were so good to them and they were good to me as well.

Terrence and Bonnie took me to the mall and bought me new clothes, toiletries, and all kinds of stuff. Bonnie even paid me for helping her taking care of Janelle's kids. I observed how blessed these three kids were to have Terrence and Bonnie caring for them during the difficult time their parents were facing in Haiti. I knew this would be a memory they would never forget.

There was never a dull moment at Terrence and Bonnie's house; the kids were always playing and running everywhere. Janelle's and Bonnie's kids were so united, it seemed like they had already known each other before. Kids don't see each other's differences; they are pure before the Lord. Jesus said in Matthew 18:3 that if we are not humbled as a little child, we cannot enter into the kingdom of Heaven. God hates a proud look (Proverbs 6:17). We should always be humbled before God so he can lift us up in due season. The Bible says in James 4:6 that God resists the proud, but gives grace to the humble. God wants us to read His word and keep it.

I stayed in Indiana for at least three months. A lot of good things happened.

I really felt that God was preparing me for the next phase of my life when I was caring for those precious children. I remember there came a time where Bonnie wanted to be alone with her family (which I understood, and I was in total agreement with her), but it had become an issue on my part because I didn't know whether I should stay in the States or leave to go back to Santo Domingo. I knew that the Lord had something there for me, because I knew that I was in the right place to meet this American guy that the Lord had told me about earlier through my vision.

I remember while I was still in Indiana that the Lord reminded me to call my principal and make peace with her just as I had promised Him. When I called her on the phone, I noticed that she didn't recognize my voice. I reminded her who I was and I also told her the purpose of my call. She was very surprised to hear how I humbled myself as I spoke to her. I told her that the Lord had healed my wounded heart and given me a new one.

It didn't matter that I was right; all that mattered was that I felt the peace of God come into my heart as soon as I released her. I didn't only release her, but I got released as well. The Lord was pleased with my course of action and He forgave me, because I forgave my principal. He accomplished His word. I felt that that grudge had kept me from turning the page to the next chapter of my life, but as soon as I obeyed the Lord, a door was opened unto me.

As I was praying and waiting upon the Lord for an answer, the Lord moved on my behalf. Piper, my long time friend and financial support (and also a preacher), had sent me an email about meeting somebody and my response was, "I don't know about this. But who is it?" He replied back and said it was Brother Mitchell, but I remember writing back to him and I told him that I knew this guy. I remember that he had prayed for me over the phone four years ago. My next question was, "Isn't he married?"

He replied, "No. He was with someone, but it didn't work out between them." I kept refusing his offer, and finally I told him that I would chat with Brother Mitchell, but without any promise. Lo and behold, God was in it and we both were blind to it. Mitchell and I began to chat through Yahoo Messenger and our conversations were all about God. It pleased me to talk to him more because he was all about the Lord. If you are a Christian out there, God in all of His goodness is supposed to be your number one subject in all conversations.

It was in the mid of May 2010 and we were still carrying on our conversation. We also talked on the phone, but it wasn't as often as we chatted online. He was computer illiterate and I had to wait upon his answers for more than three minutes. Mitchell is a man of God and also an ordained minister under the leadership of Dr. Crenshaw of Revelation Ministries. Mitchell can hear the voice of God perfectly. It was a gift that he had obtained from the Lord when he was 15 years old. He also has a very good personality. He loves God with all of his being. I remember it was on the third week of May 2010 that we both began to wonder if God was part of our conversation. Mitchell told me that he was going to inquire of the Lord about us and I told him that I was going to pray about it as well.

Is It God?

Mitchell heard from the Lord before I did. I remember I called him one Sunday afternoon and he gave me the most surprising news. He said, "You won't believe what the Lord told me about you today!"

I said, "What is it?"

He said, "The Lord told me that you were my wife..."

I said, "Really?"

He said, "Yes, really!" He continued on by saying, "That's not all."

I replied, "What else?" He said that the Lord told him to propose to me and my answer would be yes. At this point I was lost and I thought, *What if he is fabricating this whole thing?* However, something inside of me believed it. I knew it was my spirit bearing witness with his spirit, and I did feel peace about it too.

He said to me, "So, what do you say?"

I replied, "Well, if the Lord said that my answer would be yes, then it shall be as he said; but I demand a confirmation." That was my last word before we ended our phone conversation.

Mitchell then added, "All right, the Lord told me to tell you that He will speak to you." I was amazed by what this man had told me over the phone, yet I questioned myself. How could he hear God so plainly? But it was all good; it made me very happy to finally know for sure that my waiting trial had come to an end. Praise the Lord!

When I told Bonnie about it, she was extremely excited for me. She told me that she would help me plan my wedding. After a couple of hours had passed, Bonnie had changed her mind. Fear came upon her and she said, "Lina, don't you think you are to check this guy out?" I told her for some reason that I felt peace about the whole situation. I began to notice that day after day Bonnie was getting more anxious about what was going to take place. In the beginning I couldn't understand her concern for me. I thought she was trying to stop me, because she had contacted my missionary folk in Florida and told them that I was going to make a big mistake. Almost all of my orphanage brothers and sisters were against this union which God had joined together. I believe they all thought that Mitchell was an ex-con, but I didn't blame them, because they couldn't understand what God was trying to do.

I remember the story about Nicodemus. He was a Pharisee and a master of Israel, and he came to Jesus by night desiring to know who He really was. From my perception, he first wanted to hear a word from Jesus before he could make his judgment. As soon as he found out who Jesus was, then he said to the rest of the Pharisees, "Does the law judge any man, before it hears him, and know what he does?" (John 7:50-51).

We as Christians are to be careful about the judgment that we bring upon each other by looking on the outward appearance. The Bible said in Matthew 7:1-2, "Judge not, that ye be not judged. For with what judgment ye judged: and with what measure ye mete, it shall be measured back to you again." Before you decide to place a judgment upon somebody, you need to inquire of God first about this person; because if there is anybody out there who really knows about you and me it is the Lord and He will never lie to you. This is why it is very important for you and me to have an intimate relationship with him. His desire is for you to know what He knows and to be led by His Spirit.

Right before I left Bonnie's house, the Lord showed me that she was going to conceive her fourth child. When I told her about it, she said it was impossible because she had had her tubes tied. I remember quoting this scripture to her, "What is impossible with men is all possible with God," (Luke 18:27). I reminded Bonnie of the prayer request that I made to the Lord; I told her that the Lord was going to make a way for me and he did.

I was supposed to fly to South Carolina to visit one of my orphanage sisters who is also married to an American man, but when I began to think about the transition and the waiting process of this whole trip, I backed out of it. I called Mitchell that Thursday night and I asked him if he would drive to the state of Indiana to pick me up.

He told me that he would head out on the road early that weekend and he would be there by Sunday evening. I packed all my bags and was ready to go. When I thought he was getting close to Indiana, I called him to check the status of his arrival. I found out that he was still in North Carolina, and he still hadn't left yet. When I asked him why he hadn't left yet, he wasn't sure how to reply to my question. Later, after we got married, he told me that he was in doubt and that he was looking for another confirmation from the Lord.

He said the Lord spoke to him that Sunday morning while he was still in church, and the Lord told him, "You've got to go and pick your wife up and get her out of that house now." He said that he immediately started on the road that Sunday evening. It took him 13 long hours to drive from North Carolina to Indiana. When Mitchell had finally arrived in Indiana, he called to inform us that he was at the nearest McDonalds, which was 15 minutes away from us. Bonnie and I had decided to carry my suitcases to the car as we were waiting upon Terrence to arrive home so we could say our last good bye before we went to meet Mitchell.

When Terrence came home, he walked up to me and gave me a big hug, said goodbye and told me to be safe. Bonnie and I took off immediately; right after her husband came home. It only took us 15 minutes drive to get to McDonalds where Mitchell was. When we got to the place, there was my future husband waiting by his Cadillac. I remember his first words to me were, "Hi! You look nice!"

After Bonnie had introduced herself, I remember she looked at me and said, "Will you be all right?"

I replied, "Yes, I think I will be fine." Mitchell unloaded Bonnie's trunk and transferred all my suitcases into his trunk. As Mitchell and I were getting into the car, Bonnie walked over and gave me a big hug and said good-bye. Before she took off, she took a picture of both Mitchell and me. I knew why she did what she did; it was just to show everybody what Mitchell had looked like. Then again, I also think she did it because she was concerned about me.

After Bonnie had taken off, Mitchell and I started on the road to South Carolina. Inside the car he began his conversation, and he told me about himself and what he does. He said that he has been on the road travelling for the Lord. He also told me about the instructions that the Lord had given him about us.

As for me, I was so distant; I was leaning all the way over to my window. I barely said anything at the beginning of our trip. I didn't know that he had no fuel in his car, but Piper called and asked him if I was in the car with him. He said, "Yes, she is." Piper asked him about the status of the fuel in his car and I heard him say, "Not well."

I remember Bonnie had given me $50.00 for gas, so I opened up my purse and got the money out of my bag and I handed it to him. I told him that Bonnie had told me to give this to him. I heard him shout, "Praise God!" He told me that he was low on fuel and he didn't have any money left; he drove all the way to Indiana by faith, but the Lord had provided for his needs. Mitchell is a man of faith. He isn't afraid to take any risk to go wherever God sends him, despite financial issues.

There was a lot to talk, because we both were complete strangers to one another. Mitchell is from the country and is also very talkative. I'm not. I'm the quiet type whenever I want to be; but I can talk, don't get me wrong. Halfway during our road trip, I began to tell him about me and what I did. I remember it was a bit after 9:00 pm when everybody started calling his phone one by one, demanding to talk to me because they were worried about me and wanted to know if I was still alive. I told them that

I was fine and that I was still alive. After a while they had stop calling because it was getting very late.

Mitchell told me that he would make a stop at North Carolina because he was very tired and he hadn't slept for hours. When we finally arrived at his place in North Carolina, it was about 11:00 pm. Mitchell and Piper were roommates and they were staying in a pretty good-sized mobile home. It had three bedrooms, two bathrooms, a kitchen, and a living room. It was very nice and clean. It was so good to see Piper again; it had been a while since I had last seen him, but it seemed like he was happier to see me finally be in the same place as he was.

We couldn't talk too much that night — it had been a long trip and I was very tired. I told him that I would go and lay down and I would see him on the morrow. I remember that Mitchell gave me his bed and he took the couch; nothing happened between us that night. We ended up staying in his place for another day, because he was very exhausted, and it would be another 5 hours drive to South Carolina where Rosa, my orphanage sister, was staying.

The next day we got on the road again and were on our way to see Rosa. I felt bad for Mitchell because I couldn't help him drive. It took us five long hours to get to South Carolina and since we had her physical address we drove directly to her house. I remember before I got out of the car Mitchell said that the Lord told him to tell me that this neighborhood was very dangerous and I should be careful. Mitchell and I got out of the car and went knocking at her door. When she opened the door she was so happy to see me, and I was happy to see her. I introduced Mitchell to her and she introduced me to her husband, Jimmy.

That night we all sat down around the table and ate dinner together. We talked about a lot of good things. I really enjoyed Rosa's husband because he was very funny. After dinner as Mitchell was getting ready to leave, suddenly Rosa spoke up and said, "Be careful around this neighborhood; it is known to be a very dangerous place."

Mitchell and I looked at each other and I spoke up and said to her, "That was the very thing he said to me before we came into your house, because the Lord had revealed it to him." This man, the very person who was going to be my future husband, never ceases to amaze me in the way he hears from God. I believe the Lord had proved himself through Mitchell in order to let me know that he was sent from God. Mitchell left that night to go back to North Carolina, but before he left he gave me a hug and told me that he would come back for me within a week. I didn't really know how to reply to him yet, because I was still waiting upon a confirmation from the Lord. After Mitchell had left, I asked Rosa and Jimmy what they thought about Mitchell.

Not even they were in terms of agreement concerning Mitchell and me. I found myself alone in the decision that God had me to make. Sometimes when God tells you to do something, don't be surprised to find yourself alone in it.

The things which the Lord will have you to do will sometimes look foolish in the eyes of the world. This is why Paul said in 1 Corinthians 1:27, that "God hath chosen the foolish things of the world to confound the wise: and God hath chosen the weak things of the world to confound the things which are mighty." The carnal mind cannot receive the things of God (Romans 8:7). Only through the spirit can a man receive something from God. The Bible also says to walk in the spirit so that we don't fulfill the lust of the flesh (Galatians 5:16).

While in South Carolina, I was mostly alone in the house during the day because Jimmy and Rosa were working with the little kids at their church. Mitchell and I spoke on the phone every day. I remember he kept on inquiring if the Lord had not yet spoken to me. I told him that He hadn't yet, but I was still praying about it. Jimmy and Rosa took me to a summer play one weekend night; it was very entertaining and I really enjoyed myself.

Rosa had given me some instructions about the ADT security system inside the pastor's house where they were staying. She told me not to open the door if I was still inside the house, because the alarm would go off. It happened on a day when I had totally forgotten about what she said. I went to the door, grabbed the door knob, and opened it. Immediately the alarm went off, and the police showed up and were knocking at the door. When I went to get the door they asked me if something was wrong. I told them it was an accident and they understood, and assured me that these things happen all the time. They told me that I should just be mindful about it next time. It was so embarrassing. When Jimmy and Rosa came home that afternoon, I told them about it and they both looked at each other and busted out laughing; we ended up having a wonderful evening together that day.

It was God!

I remember during the third day of the week, I went to bed that night and woke up at 2 in the morning to use the bathroom. I then walked back to my room and knelt down before my bed and began to pray. I began to ask God when He would speak to me and tell me who this Mitchell was. That very night — I can't tell whether I was asleep or awake — a vision came to me.

In my vision, I was in a place by myself. I remember there was a mattress on the floor and I was sitting on it. I also had a laptop in my hands and I was browsing through the Internet. All of a sudden, I fell asleep. After a couple of minutes, I woke up and I discovered that the door was half opened and the light had been turned off. The strange thing was that before I fell asleep, the door was shut and the light was on. I couldn't understand what was happening.

I got up to close the door and I saw a huge rat inside the room. It must have come in after I fell asleep. I set my eyes on that rat and I commanded it to leave, and suddenly that rat ran out the door and it was gone. Jesus said that He gave us power to tread on serpents and scorpions, and over all the powers of the enemy, and nothing shall by any means hurt you (Luke 10:19). We believers have to start using the power that is within us; no longer does the devil have any power over you. He only has power over you if you allow him to have it.

Still in my vision, after I had closed the door and I reached out to pull the light switch on, I heard a voice. It was an audible voice, and it was loud and clear. The first word that I heard was, "Hey." It startled me to the point where I became mute and I didn't know how to reply to it. After several minutes, it came to my spirit what Mitchell had told me. He told me that the Lord was going to speak to me and he said that, when He did, to ask the Lord what He would have me to do. So I did. I quickly asked the Lord what He wanted me to do.

He replied, "I want you to go to Pastor Dean's. He will give you a fresh bottle of coke and you will take it to Mitchell."

I said, "All right, but who is Pastor Dean?" The Lord sent a young man to lead me to Pastor Dean's house, and while we were on the road to Pastor Dean's I woke up. I thanked the Lord so much for providing me with the confirmation I was looking for; I praised Him.

I was so excited because I knew that it wasn't any man that spoke to me; it was the Lord. Although men had rejected God's choice between Mitchell and me, it didn't stop God because He will have His way in everything. I love all of my family and friends, but I can't please them. We all have a walk to walk and each of our walks is different from each other. I ought to obey God rather than men.

I know Mitchell wasn't what everyone had expected, but he is the best husband that the Lord could've ever given me. He has the God quality and that is sufficient for me. I didn't choose him and he didn't choose me. The Lord joined us together for the ministry. I couldn't wait to call him and tell him that the Lord had finally spoken to me.

I called him that day, but I couldn't get through. When he called back, before I even said anything, he told me that the Lord told him that I knew now who he was. I answered, "Yes I do, but I've got one more question to ask."

He said, "What is it?"

I said, "Who is Pastor Dean?" The moment I asked him about Pastor Dean, he started laughing through the phone. He said that he had the rest of my vision and he would tell me about it later when he picked me up.

I told Rosa what the Lord had spoken to me concerning Mitchell and that he was the one. I also told her that now I knew for sure that I was going to be married to Mitchell from West Virginia. After the week was over I said good-bye to Rosa and her husband and hello to my future hubby.

I remember the first thing I inquired of Mitchell about was Pastor Dean, and he made the most shocking statement. He said, "I am Pastor Dean. The Lord gave you my middle name." He rejoiced saying, "How amazing!" Mitchell told me that four years ago the Lord spoke to him and told him that he had called him to be a pastor, and his name would be Pastor Dean. The Lord had not only mentioned his first name to me, but He also revealed his middle name as well. Wow! What a mighty God I serve; He is so real. We were heading back to North Carolina as happy as we could be; unaware of the ongoing trial that was awaiting us. God help us!

When we arrived home later that evening, Mitchell said he had a surprise for me. He went inside his bedroom and came out with a little gift box in his hand. When he opened it, it was the most beautiful engagement ring that I had ever seen. Right there he went on his knees and proposed to me. Just as the Lord said, it happened.

The next day Mitchell went out to speak to couple of the pastors that he knew and wanted to know if they would marry us. Both of them said that before they married us we'd have to sit under their leadership, which could take at least six months. The Lord told Mitchell not to tarry on our wedding, but to do it immediately. Men say one thing, but the Lord says another. Which would you choose? I think we humans sometimes think we know better than God, but we're so wrong. That's why the Lord says in Isaiah 55:8-9, "For my thoughts are not your thoughts, neither are your ways my ways. And as the heavens are higher than the earth, so are my ways higher than your ways and my thoughts than your thoughts, declares the Lord."

Within a week and a half on May 3, 2010 we went down to the court house of Wilkesboro, NC and tied the knot with Piper and his girlfriend as the two witnesses. Mitchell and I were happily married in the Lord. We couldn't afford to go on our honeymoon, so we went back home. A month and a half later, Piper had moved out of the house and we were left with a bill to pay. Mitchell had managed to pay the bill by making candies and selling them.

I remember about three weeks after we got married, Mitchell had a night vision. In his vision the Lord was speaking to him, but he was talking back to the Lord in a loud voice. I woke up and found out that he had been talking in his sleep. I could hear everything he was saying, but one thing he said stood out, "Lina, pray."

He continued on his conversation with the Lord in his sleep and I heard him say, "I can't go down that road." The Lord kept insisting for him to go down that road, but he kept refusing, and finally the word of the Lord had prevailed against his, and he went down the road. I heard him say again, "Lina, pray." I decided to wake him up out his sleep and asked him questions concerning the vision he had.

He told me that we were driving upon this terrible road, he said it was the roughest road that he had ever seen in his life, but lo and behold this was the very path that the Lord had wanted us to go through. Mitchell said that when he had finally driven down that road, one of the front tires went completely flat.

He spoke up and said, "Now what are we going to do? Look, we're stranded." For some reason, he said that I started laughing and he couldn't understand why I was laughing in the middle of a crisis. In the vision, while we were both waiting in the middle of nowhere, a big truck loaded with big tires showed up out of nowhere and came to our rescue.

Mitchell said there were three men who had gotten out of the truck filled with tires. The men then took out one of the tires from their truck and changed our front tire, and we were moving again. After they had fixed our tire, they vanished. Mitchell said we no longer had any more car trouble, and then we finally drove into a smoother path.

This vision plainly described the trial and tribulation that was ahead of us. God will only let you go but so far in your trials; He will deliver you, and will also give you peace in the middle of the storm; He will also bring you out. He said in the world we shall have tribulation, but be of good cheer for I have overcome the world (John 16:33). Our trials and tribulation are temporary, but the things we can't see with our eyes are eternal.

Sometimes God will allow us to go through a situation that would seem so unfair in our eyes, but lo and behold, we have no idea how much He will use that situation to bless us with double.

Mitchell and I struggled a lot. There were days in which we went without food, and God sent the landlord to our door during those days to buy us groceries. Mitchell had taught me how to go on a real fast. I used to fast for half a day, but he taught me to go all the way. My longest fast was three full days without food.

Fasting is very important. If you're looking for God to make a drastic change in your life, it requires a fast. If you're looking for deliverance in your body or you desire for a member of your family to get delivered, or if you want God to move quickly in your situation, sometimes it requires a little bit more than prayer. It requires a fast. We can't be expecting God to do so much when we're offering just a little bit. I guarantee you — when you start fasting, you will hear from God.

Samuel told Saul, "Hath the Lord has great delight in burnt offerings and sacrifices, as in obeying the voice of the Lord? Behold, to obey is better than sacrifice," (1 Samuel 15:22).

God is our heavenly Father and He loves us with an everlasting love. He sent His only begotten son, Jesus, to die on the cross for you and me. If you have studied about the life of Jesus when He used to walk this earth, He walked in all obedience with the Father until the day He went to the cross. That's why the voice of God came from Heaven when Jesus was baptizing at the Jordan River under the leadership of John the Baptist and said, "This is my beloved Son, in whom I am well pleased, hear him," (Luke 9:35).

The life of Jesus Christ should be a great example to us believers today and the only way you could please God the Father is by obeying the voice of His son, Jesus Christ. Jesus said "My sheep hear my voice, and a stranger they will not follow."

You may be asking yourself, "How can one hear God's voice?" It's simple: by accepting Him into your heart as your Lord and Savior and beginning a relationship with Him today.

THE BEGINNING OF OUR TRIALS

Mitchell and I lived in North Carolina for about six months. One day while we both were praying for instructions from the Lord, the Lord gave me a vision. In that vision I heard a voice whisper to me that after we were married we were supposed to go to West Virginia. As I was waking up, I could hear the echo of that voice in my spirit saying, "West Virginia."

In the morning, I said to Mitchell that I knew where we're supposed to go and he replied, "Where?"

I said, "West Virginia,"

He replied back, "Not again." I didn't really know why he despised his home town so much, but I was getting ready to find out. He lingered as much as he could to hear from the Lord himself, because he didn't want to go back to West Virginia. He is the only Christian in his family and therefore they despised him, and now they really think that he has lost it, because he has married me.

Five months later, the Lord spoke to Mitchell and told him that He was sending him to his hometown. It was at the end of October 2010 when we left North Carolina to go to West Virginia. When we left, we only had a total of $50.00 in our pockets. Mitchell had contacted one of his brothers, Caleb, who lives in West Virginia to make some arrangements concerning a place for us to stay. He told Mitchell to come on down.

We started on the road that Saturday evening and it took us four hours to get to West Virginia. Mitchell's brother had a very small place; it was enough for him and his daughter. Thank God his daughter had been gone for few days, or we wouldn't have had a place to lay our head. When she had finally made it back home, I overheard her saying to Mitchell that their apartment was too small. I knew she wanted us to leave. I didn't blame her because she was right. I suggested to Mitchell to do what his niece had required. I told her that we would sleep in our car, because I knew that Mitchell was worried about me. This was the beginning of our trial. We were homeless for about eight days and thank the Lord Mitchell had a car.

You can imagine how hard and uncomfortable it was for both of us in that time. We had to spend the night in the car, but we would go into his brother's apartment every day to take a shower. We had been praying for the Lord to make a way for us, and He did. After being homeless for eight days, the Lord spoke to Mitchell and told him to go to a widow named Peggy. We drove to her place that afternoon and Mitchell told her about our situation and he also told her that the Lord had sent him to her house. Peggy was a long time Pentecostal preacher she was 94 years old. She also had a church.

She had never born any children, but she was a very good person. She invited us to stay over in her home until further notice from the Lord. When we got into her place, we found it was a big house but it was very dirty. Everything was out of place, the odor of cat waste had filled the atmosphere and also there were leaks almost everywhere in the house. There were dirty dishes everywhere on the kitchen counter; only God knows how long these dishes had been lying there. I can understand; two old women. They were both widows and they were also sisters.

We immediately knew what we had to do. We couldn't start cleaning that same day, because we were both exhausted and we had to rest, but the next day we began a general cleaning and dusting everywhere around the house. We also washed all the dishes. After we had finished our chores, Peggy came and inspected her house; she was amazed at the transformation that had taken place in her home. Even her family was surprised by what they saw when they came to check on her; they expressed their gratitude. Not only did we clean, dust, and wash dishes, we also cooked for them. They really enjoyed our hospitality.

In the book of (James 1:27), James spoke of the perfect example of true Christianity. He said, "Pure and undefiled religion in the sight of God is this, to visit the fatherless and widows in their affliction, and to keep oneself unspotted from the world." We have to be careful how we live our lives before God, because He is watching; everything we do is being recorded. The word of God tells us how we need to live a perfect life before God. Read your Bible every day and pray daily, and let the Holy Spirit guide you and lead you in the way that you are to go.

We had been in Peggy's church a couple of times; it was a nice church. The Lord spoke to Mitchell and told him to start a revival. Mitchell and another preacher went from church to church posting flyers on every door. On the first day of the revival, we had a good-sized congregation. Mitchell preached an awesome word that night, and the Lord moved mightily through the service. The second day likewise, we had another great service, and the presence of God was there. We had invited Joshua, my orphanage brother, to preach on the last day of the revival. We had an awesome night in the Lord. Joshua preached a powerful message that night and the Spirit of the Lord ministered to many hearts. We give God all the glory, honor, and the praise for the wonderful things He has done.

After staying in Peggy's house for two full months, her family started wondering when we were going to move out. The Lord spoke to Mitchell and told him that it was time to leave, not knowing where we should be afterwards. We packed our bags that day and we left.

We hadn't had any instructions from the Lord yet and we ended up sleeping in our car for a few days. There was this particular pastor with whom we had gotten acquainted; his name was Pastor Derek. The Lord told Mitchell to give him a call and tell him about our situation. He was moved by our situation and he told us to come down and meet him at his church. We did and when we got there he encouraged us through the word and said, "This trial will soon be over." I hoped and wished it was true, but we thanked him for his encouragement.

He had a second house; it was an old, abandoned place. He prepared us a room so we could lay our heads. It was the beginning of December 2010; you can imagine how cold it was. There was no heat, and no water whatsoever. Inside that room we praised and worshipped the Lord every day. We had an electric heater, but it was impossible to heat up the whole room. We had two big blankets, but still the cold air remained the same in our room. The good thing was that we didn't have to spend the day in that cold room; we only had to spend the night there. Pastor Derek and his wife were good people; I think they had done their duty which was required of them. We attended their church and we enjoyed the service each time we had an opportunity to be part of it. They had a big congregation.

I remember one time while Mitchell and I were helping with some things in the church, I felt led to call Joshua. When I did, he gave me the most amazing news. He told me that Bonnie was pregnant and I shouted, "Hallelujah, glory be unto God!" The word of the Lord had come to pass. I told Joshua that before I left Bonnie's house the Lord had told me to tell her that she was going to conceive again, but she didn't believe it.

You see, even when we don't believe in the word of God, it cannot hinder the word to prosper, because God is not a man that He should lie. In Isaiah 55:11, we can see how God defends His word when He said, "So shall my word be that goeth forth out of my mouth: it shall not return unto me void, but it shall accomplish that which I please, and it shall prosper in the thing whereto I sent it."

A great example of this scripture was when Zacharias the priest's wife Elizabeth was barren. It happened on a day while he executed his duty before the Lord, an angel of the Lord appeared unto him and told him that his wife was going to conceive a child, but being the high priest that he was in that time, he doubted the word of the Lord. Did his unbelief stop the word of God from coming to pass? God forbid. Instead, he went mute for nine full months until the day the word of the Lord had been accomplished in his wife Elizabeth (Luke 1).

Our unbelief cannot hinder the word of God to prosper, "For the word of God is quick, and powerful, and sharper than any two-edged sword, piercing even to the dividing asunder of soul and spirit, and of the joints and marrow, and is a discerner of the thoughts and intents of the heart," (Hebrews 4:12). We believers need to know that the weapons of our warfare are not carnal, but mighty through God to the pulling down of strongholds, (2 Corinthians 10:4).

I remember it was on a weekend night; Pastor Derek had a sleep over in the church. It was a good night. We watched a Christian movie, we ate and we played games. We did everything but pray. Later that night, when we were all sound asleep, a vision came to me.

In my vision, there was something going on outside the church, and I saw a spirit came through the church door and enter inside the building. I couldn't describe his appearance, because he had a black hood on, and nothing but darkness encamped it. After everyone had run out of the church to see what was happening in the street, that spirit moved closer and closer to me. Then I knew that it was evil. Mitchell was still standing there with me while everybody was gone, but after a while he went out of the church, and I was left alone inside the church with that evil spirit.

I knew that he had come for me, but I also knew that he had no power over me. As the evil spirit was approaching me, I heard the Lord spoke, and He said, "Lina hasn't prayed yet, but when she does you will see what's going to happen." As soon as the evil spirit heard the voice of the Lord, he quickly took off and ran out of the church. As I was chasing after it, I began to pray and declare the word of God. These are the very words that I prayed and declared upon that evil spirit: I began to call the lightning from Heaven to strike that spirit and immediately it was struck and had fallen down.

Now, the Lord isn't saying for us to make that kind of prayer and declaration against flesh and blood, but against principalities, against powers, against rulers of the darkness of this world, and against spiritual wickedness in high places (Ephesians 6:12). That's why we believers have to commit ourselves to prayer every day, because there is a spiritual war taking place on our behalf in the high places.

After a month and a half, Mitchell found a painting job (Mitchell is also a professional painter). In January 2011, we moved out of that cold room into a 3-bedroom apartment. It was a very nice place; it was big and very spacious.

Now I understand in what context Paul said, "I know both how to be abased, and I know how to abound," (Philippians 4:12). Paul also said in Philippians 4:11, "Not that I speak in respect of want, for I have learned in whatsoever state I am, therewith to be content." God literally poured out his blessings upon us in that particular time, but it didn't last for very long. I believe the Lord had given us a break from our trial, because there was more to come.

We lived three full months in abundance. The lady that Mitchell worked for was very wealthy. She supplied us with some expensive furniture for our apartment. Within four months we had to move out of that apartment, because we couldn't afford to pay the rent, and also Mitchell's painting contract was over. In the meantime, Mitchell applied for government housing, but we couldn't move in yet.

The Lord told Mitchell that He was sending us to the Thomas' home, and Mrs. Thomas already knew that we were coming, because the Lord had told her. They were a Christian couple who used to attend the same church as we did. They were very good people; they supplied our needs. We were not aware of the reason why the Lord had wanted us to stay in their place, but we would soon find out.

I can say it was very difficult for me to have to go through this. That was probably the hardest thing in our trial that God could've ever required of me. I love my privacy, but sometimes God will remove you out of your comfort zone and place you where he wants you to be. Jesus said in Matthew 18:12, "Will you leave the 99 and go after the one?" I had to surrender to the will of God, although I battled in my flesh so hard to get out of it.

When we moved in the Thomas' home, everything and everyone seemed perfectly fine. However, within a couple of weeks of our stay in their home, Mr. Thomas pulled Mitchell to the side and began to tell him many things that were going wrong in their place. He told Mitchell that his wife was the main problem, but I found it hard to understand, because she seemed like the most spiritual person that I had ever met. 2 Corinthians 11:14 warns us about how Satan himself is transformed into an angel of light, but the Spirit of the Lord reveals the hidden things. Mr. Thomas told Mitchell that was the very reason why he was slipping away from the Lord and he had stopped going to church. Every day, Mr. Thomas would get together with Mitchell and begin to reveal more things that were happening inside his home.

I remember it was on a Friday morning when the Lord spoke to Mitchell and told him to go get a building and start a revival. Mitchell got up that morning and told the Thomas' concerning the instruction which the Lord had given him. The Thomas' had already begun a prayer meeting in their home before we came. That particular morning, Mrs. Thomas began to call the members of her prayer meeting to contribute their share to the building.

We were still short of more money, but Mitchell had contributed his whole income to the building. Mitchell called the owner of the building and told her that we were ready to get the building. The owner gave Mitchell an appointment to meet him there. Mitchell and the pastor of the prayer meeting went down to meet with the owner. She agreed to rent them the building. She made the most amazing statement and said, "I have never done this before for anyone," but because Mitchell and the pastor were going to convert this building into a church, she wouldn't charge them a deposit. Now that was God, and Mitchell knew it was a confirmation that God had spoken to him.

A couple of weeks later, Mitchell and I began to notice the things that were spoken by Mr. Thomas. Mrs. Thomas became our enemy inside her own home, because she thought we were on her husband's side. Mitchell and I had started a three day fast to bind the spirit that was trying to destroy their marriage, but it seemed like it was getting worse and worse because Mrs. Thomas would not stop. It became a constant issue; day after day we were being persecuted.

The same day that the building was released to us, we cleaned and mopped the entire place. The Lord supplied everything. A church had donated some of their church pews to our church; another pastor from another church had brought a sound system and given it to our church. I made a big "Holy Ghost Revival" sign to go on the front top of the building and we offered our thanksgiving and dedicated the building to the Lord.

That night we started our first night revival and the presence and the power of God was present in that place. It felt like the ark of the Lord was in this place; we were getting filled with His anointing every night. The power of God was so strong in that building, it could have raised the dead. We were getting drunk and elevated in His Spirit every night.

On a particular night as Mitchell was singing and playing the guitar and leading the service, the power and the fire of the Holy Ghost was present. I remember there was this particular woman who had never been in church before, but when she came to our church that night she fell under the power of God. As she was lying on the floor I walked up to her and put my hands on her hands and I declared to her, "Receive ye the Holy Ghost!" Immediately, she began to speak in new tongues. It was nothing I did; it was the Lord who had filled her with his Spirit.

The revival went on and on while the devil was getting more and more aggravated. We began to experience oppositions on every side, but the presence and the power of God had multiplied. It was close to Christmas Eve when things had begun to stir up inside the home of the Thomas family.

Mr. Thomas had been drinking secretly because he couldn't take the pressure any more. He had two guns hidden inside the house. When he got very drunk and was determined to end his life, his wife and daughter went and removed the guns from their place and hid them in another place. I remember when Mr. Thomas came inside the house looking for the guns, he couldn't find them. When he went back outside to drink some more, Mitchell went after him and began to minister to him again. When Mr. Thomas had finally come to himself, he repented to the Lord and to his family and made a vow to the Lord that he would never go back to this drinking habit again. Mr. Thomas had started to come to the revival and he was refreshed by the power and the presence of the Lord. Praise the Lord for another great miracle that He had done! Our mission was accomplished.

The Lord spoke to Mitchell and told him that our time was expired at the Thomas home. We went to take refuge in the church, but the oppositions and persecutions were still on, and Mrs. Thomas was one of them. We had such an awesome experience of the power of God in that church every night.

I remember on a regular night while we were praising the Lord, I began to experience something in the spirit that I had never felt before — my hands were on fire. It wasn't any natural fire, but it was the fire of the Holy Ghost. There were flames of fire all over my hands which my physical eyes couldn't see, but I know what was happening to me in the spirit. I felt like it was part of me, and it is a part of me, because ever since my first experience with the fire it has never ceased to manifest upon me. The Lord told me that this fire was a gift that He gave to both Mitchell and me to touch the world.

Dear readers, the power that the world is longing to possess does not come from the outside. It is hidden on the inside, but you can't get any access to it unless it is through the giver, the Lord Jesus Christ. God owns all power and has all authority, but He has delivered it unto His people to take possession of it. The more persecutions and oppositions we experienced, the more the power of God did abound. On a special night while we were praising and worshipping the Lord, we discovered a mist had been all over the building; it was the Shekinah glory.

We began to shout and glorify God for His glory that was seen in that place.

Mrs. Thomas and some of her relatives brought a lot of confusion in the middle of the revival meetings. It happened on the 90th day of the revival that the Lord spoke to Mitchell and told him to shut down the revival. Mitchell and I were very exhausted after that 90 day revival, but it paid off. After the revival was over, Mitchell and I prayed for instructions from the Lord.

We already knew that the Lord was sending us to Texas, but we didn't know which part of Texas. I remember it was on December 18, 2010 when the Lord gave me a clear vision about this woman who had a church, but I was also sitting in her congregation and people were testifying one by one. I stood up and testified, but while I was testifying about how the Lord had saved my life from the earthquake that hit my country, the Spirit of the Lord came upon me so strongly and I heard the woman's first and last name, and who she was. The name that I heard was Jael and that she was a prophetess.

I woke up that morning and I told Mitchell about the vision, but it wasn't until two days later while we were still wondering where in Texas we needed to be that I began to wonder about my vision. I went online and began to look for the woman that I saw in my vision. I was amazed by what I had discovered; there appeared on my screen the exact profile, and the first and last name of the woman that I saw in my vision. When I read her information, it said that she was a prophetess and lived in Lancaster, Texas. Now what the Lord had really wanted to show me was the city in which we had to be in; it was Lancaster. I'm so in awe with my God; He is so real and I love Him with all of my heart. He will not let you be deceived.

We were so excited about the information that the Lord had revealed to us that day, but we had no idea of the extent of the ongoing trials and tribulations that were going to take place in Texas. We thought we went through a trial in West Virginia, but it was nothing compared to what was going to happen in Texas. Sometimes God will tell you about all the good parts, but He leaves out the middle part where you have to walk through your trials and tribulation. But you know what? He's still going to be with you through it all. Remember His word in Deuteronomy 31:8, when He said that He'll never leave you nor forsake you, but he will always bring you through your circumstances.

Detour on the road to Texas

I remember before we left for Texas, the Lord spoke to Mitchell and told him to go to New York. Mitchell called the pastor of the church and told him about our departure. He also gave him some basic instructions about the church. We were so happy to leave the state of West Virginia. Melia had been expecting us, because she took interest in our furniture and decided to buy it. Her husband had sent some money so we could rent a truck to bring their furniture to New York. Mitchell went to the truck company and rented a Budget truck; that's how we were able to make it to New York.

It was January 2013; it was a very cold day and a long trip. We started on the road that Friday night and we made it to New York the next day. We were so exhausted. I called Melia and told her that we had arrived and were waiting in front of her apartment. When she finally came down to open the door, we were both delighted to see each other again. I introduced Mitchell to her, but her husband had not made it home yet; he was still at work. I also met her children, who were both adorable.

There were a couple of things that happened while we were in New York. Melia's landlord lived on the first floor with his two sons. We never met him, but his two sons were drug addicts; therefore they had created a lot of trouble in the area. We prayed every day for a change to take place downstairs, but it hadn't happened yet. I thanked God that He was watching over this family, but I also thanked God because He protected us during our stay in their home. I remember before we left New York to go to Texas, Mitchell went out one day, and he didn't come home until noon. He was so excited when he came home and he told me he had found a good church we could attend. The next day we took a bus to the church. I really enjoyed the service and the presence of God in that place.

The presence and the anointing of God was so strong in that place, the pastor began to prophesy to several people in the church. Pastor Wonder was his name; he was a powerful man of God. He called Mitchell and me to come up front and he began to prophesy to us. I remember he asked me if I had any children, and I said no. He continued on prophesying and said to me, "The Lord said you're going to have twins when the time is right." Mitchell and I looked at each other and smiled, but Mitchell spoke up and told the pastor that the Lord had already provided me with two names. The pastor was very amazed and said, "Do you hear that, church? The Lord is speaking." It was a confirmation to the pastor that the Lord had spoken to him.

He prophesied many other things to us and told us that there was a church waiting for us in Texas. I remember Pastor Wonder asked Mitchell when we were leaving New York and Mitchell spoke up and said, "Tomorrow." The pastor and his church gave us a love offering for our bus fare and that's how we were able to make it to Texas.

ALONE IN THE LONE STAR STATE

It was March 2013 when we rode for two days on the greyhound bus. You're talking about fatigue — we were exhausted beyond measure. After we had arrived at the bus station, we sat down and waited. I remember asking Mitchell what the holdup was. He spoke up and said that he was waiting on the Lord to speak to him. After 15 minutes, the Lord spoke to Mitchell and told him to go to Motel 6 in Lancaster. We called a taxi right away and we told the driver to take us to Motel 6. It was 2 in the morning when he had dropped us off with our suitcases in our hands.

Mitchell went to sign us up for a room, but the motel manager told us that all the rooms were full. He told us to come back in the morning around 9 am. Mitchell told him that we needed a place to put our bags and suitcases, because we didn't have a vehicle. The manager opened the office door and took our luggage until we returned in the morning.

In the meantime, we walked to a Waffle House that was nearby the motel. We ate breakfast and sat there and talked about our trip; we tarried there until it was the breaking of day. When we finally walked out of the Waffle House it was still early, so we decided to make a small tour. Around 9 am, we walked back to the motel and there was a room waiting for us.

We entered into the room, laid our luggage on the floor, mounted up the bed and fell fast asleep. I remember on our very first night in the motel, I had a vision. In my vision I saw a man in a white van that had come for us and as we were getting ready to enter inside his van the enemy tried to stop us. I took action against the enemy and I rebuked him and immediately we were able to leave that place.

The enemy has no power over us. In Isaiah 54:17 it says, "No weapon that is formed against thee shall prosper: and every tongue that shall rise against thee in judgment thou shall condemn." This is the heritage of the servants of the Lord, and their righteousness is of me, saith the Lord. You see, God is on our side. He said if He be for you, who can be against you? (Romans 8:31). The Lord has given us the authority over all the power of the enemy; therefore we have to start using that power. That power is the word of God. When you pray and read your Bible daily, then the devil can't mess with you. The Bible said in 2 Corinthians 10:4, "For the weapons of our warfare are not carnal, but mighty through God to the pulling down of strongholds."

We had been praying and seeking God's face ever since we came down to the motel. We were also running out of money; but I couldn't doubt the Lord, because I knew what He had showed me and I had to stand on His word. Our time was running out and we had been there for eight days already. The Lord spoke to Mitchell and told him to get out and go look for the church. Mitchell didn't know anyone in Texas or even which way to go, so he went out walking.

I remember it was around noon when Mitchell came back to the motel, but he wasn't alone. He was with the man in the white van that the Lord had showed me the week before. I came out to meet him and he introduced himself as Mr. Lens.

After a while, we both got into his van and he took us to the church. It only took us five minutes to get there, but we were so surprised how close we were to the church and we weren't even aware of it. The Lord had placed us in the right position. The church was on the other side of the street across from Motel 6. Wow, God is so amazing! When we got to the church, Mr. Lens opened up the door and we walked inside the building and he showed us the sanctuary. He told us that the church had been vandalized and the thieves who broke into the building had spread chemicals all over the carpet. Therefore, the church had remained closed for about 6 months. When I walked in the sanctuary, it reminded me of the church that I had seen previously in one of my many visions while I was in New York.

In that particular vision, Mitchell and I, Melia and her husband were inside a big place and there was a waiting line where people were getting food and drinks. I came into the sanctuary area and just stood there observing the place, when all of a sudden the Lord opened up my eyes and I saw angels among us who were clothed in white raiment and they were all over the sanctuary. Some of them were praising God with their hands lifted up in the air, while others were doing some type of cleansing. There was one in particular who was sitting in the water inside the water baptism basin. As glorious as the view was, it was gone suddenly.

God desires for us to see things in the spiritual realm. There is a place in the Spirit where you can determine what the future holds. John 16:13 mentions it: "Howbeit when he, the Spirit of truth is come, he will guide you into all truth: for he shall not speak of himself; but whatsoever he shall hear, that shall he speak: and he will show you things to come." God is so real and He loves you with an everlasting love. If you desire to see or hear Him, He will make Himself known unto you as He did in the past to the saints and prophets of old.

Mitchell told Mr. Lens that the Lord said to start a revival immediately and Mr. Lens replied that the only way we could get it started was if a miracle took place. Mitchell told him we would pray about it that same day.

I remember Mr. Lens asked if we had anything to eat and he reached into his pocket and handed fifty dollars to Mitchell. After he drove us back to the motel that evening, he told us that he was going out of town for a few days and that he had us covered for a few more days. Mr. Lens said when he returned he would contact us. Mitchell and I began to pray and thanked the Lord because He didn't leave us stranded. We were also praying that the Lord would open the church door to start the revival.

After a few days had gone by we didn't hear from Mr. Lens, as he had promised. Mitchell was getting a little bit worried because of me. That morning he got into the word and began to search the scriptures, and the Lord gave him this scripture in Acts 18: 9-10 which states, "then spake the Lord to Paul in the night by a vision, be not afraid, but speak, and hold not thy peace: for I am with thee, and no man shall set on thee to hurt thee: for I have much people in this city." The Lord spoke to Mitchell and told him to call Mr. Lens and gave him that scripture.

Mitchell called him and did according to the word of the Lord and he delivered the scripture to Mr. Lens. After Mr. Lens had heard the word of the Lord, he told Mitchell that he was actually driving by a place in

Glenn Heights which had a rental sign on it, but he said that he was going to speak to the landlord about it. He also told Mitchell that this place would be more convenient for us. This is the actual place where we live right now. We thanked the Lord for His word.

The next day, Mr. Lens called Mitchell and gave him some good news about the church. He said he got a letter in the mail from his insurance and they said he could go ahead and re-open the building. He also told Mitchell that we had to leave the motel that day. He told us to get our stuff ready, because he was coming to pick us up to see the new place. He showed up about an hour later, we hopped in his van and he drove us to the place. When we got there the landlord was not present, so we waited there until she had returned. That same day Mr. Lens signed the lease with both of our signatures on it, and he also took care of the deposit.

Mitchell took over the payment on the second month of April 2013, and since then our needs have been met. We saw how God poured out His blessings upon Mr. Lens because of us. He was getting blessed from left to right. Mr. Lens even confessed to us that ever since we had come to him, everything he touched had turned into gold and he would always say, "I thank God for you guys." He kept expressing his excitement about the revival to Mitchell, but we soon found out what the excitement was all about. I remember Mr. Lens drove by every morning at an early hour to pick up Mitchell and take him to the church.

Mitchell had done a lot of work in the building, but he didn't get paid. It didn't
matter anyway, because he had done it unto the Lord. Mr. Lens had the carpet removed off of the wooden floor and Mitchell painted the entire floor with red paint. He did an excellent job. Afterward, Mr. Lens had 70 purple chairs donated to the church and he went and bought a single sound speaker to complete the sanctuary.

I remember as soon as the revival got started, Mr. Lens started his own business in the building, but something regarding Mr. Lens had begun to transpire somewhere in the midst of all the excitement. Although Mr. Lens was the man in charge of the building, he wasn't a Christian; he was a backslider. Now we began to discover why the Lord had sent us to this man.

I had seen how hard Mitchell had worked for this man, but he never paid him anything. Mr. Lens was well aware of our situation. He knew we didn't have any food or water, but he had decided not to pay attention to our needs, and because of his ignorance our trial began to intensify. Mitchell had to be in the church from early in the morning until sometime in the afternoon. There were times when Mitchell would come home exhausted, and when I would ask him if Mr. Lens paid him that day his answer would always be, "No."

After Mr. Lens had the flyers made up, Mitchell and I went everywhere to pass them around. I remember Mr. Lens had made a statement to Mitchell after the sanctuary was opened for revival. He said, "You do your thing while I do my own." Mr. Lens was also in charge of a program called the C.E.O program. He was working with young people who had been in trouble with the law, especially the young men who had been in jail and those who were on probation. He was trying to keep them busy so they would stay out of trouble, but there was one thing about it that had made no sense to me. The most important thing that these young people had needed in their lives was stolen from them.

Mr. Lens had hindered these kids from coming to the revival meetings so they wouldn't be saved. There was so much confusion about this whole situation. We could admit that Mr. Lens was doing a good job, but was it enough in the eyes of God? Day after day Mitchell and I began to discover another side of Mr. Lens. It seemed like to me it had to do with a color-related issue.

In the state of Texas, especially on the north side of Texas, the level of racism is very high. The blacks are against the whites and the whites are against the blacks, as well. What is this? God did not create a divided nation and He certainly did not create a confused world. We are all brothers and sisters in the Lord, and we all have one Father which is in Heaven and He has commanded us to love one another.

After God had created every different nation and tongue in His image and in His likeness in the book of Genesis, He was well pleased with his works. While we're sitting and watching the enemy having a hay-day destroying our family and our nation, why don't we all come together in unity as one nation under God and put the devil out? There's only one way we can do this, and it's through the word *love*. 1 Corinthians chapter thirteen talks all about it. Wherever you are in your home, you can reach to your Bible and start reading 1 Corinthians 13 and while you are at it, ask the Lord to pour more love into your heart so you can make a difference.

Let us all defeat the enemy through the love of God. Amen. The Bible says in 1 Corinthians 14:33 that God isn't the author of confusion, but of peace. Confusion comes from the devil and he is the author of it. If you're experiencing any type of confusion in your life right now, notice it didn't come from God. You've got to rebuke the devil immediately and he will flee from you.

Mitchell and I faced so many setbacks and oppositions throughout the entire revival. We noticed that the people weren't coming and we began to get discouraged. It was very frustrating, especially after we had prayed over and over for this revival and fasted before the Lord. Mr. Lens was our main problem and there was a lot of confusion surrounding him. Mr. Lens wasn't interested in the revival at all; it was all about his agenda. Out of 70 days of revival meetings, Mr. Lens only showed up twice.

I remember while his business was flourishing, the revival meetings were going slowly because the people who were invited had not been coming. I remember he kept telling us that the people were coming; it sounded to me as if he was mocking. I remember telling Mitchell, "If the people don't start coming after a month, then we will end the revival." The Lord spoke to Mitchell and told him that there were some people coming. On a particular night while Mitchell and I were praying in the church, we saw three men in black walking into the sanctuary. After Mitchell had started the service, he invited the men to come one by one and share their testimonies. We had a good service that night, and the people started to come on the second week of May 2013, just as the Lord had said.

It was strange; that same night after the service was over the three men in black who had professed to be preachers of the gospel told us that they were invited by Mr. Lens. They said Mr. Lens met them at a restaurant where they were ministering the word of God to the people.

That wasn't all; they also said that Mr. Lens had given them permission to take over the revival. When Mitchell confronted Mr. Lens concerning this matter, he denied it. Mr. Lens created much confusion between us and the three preachers.

I remember when they showed up the next day, they tried to take over the revival and lead the service their own way. They began to bring their own people along. I remember they mentioned something about tithes and offerings, but we told them that in the flyers it said no tithes and offerings were allowed. The three preachers didn't accept the things that were going on in the revival meetings because they were all about the money. Therefore they created a conflict between them and us. I looked at Mitchell and I said to him, "Is this what we prayed for?"

I remember after we met Jael and got acquainted with her, I invited her to come to the revival and she said she would advise me and let me know when she was able to come. Jael was the woman the Lord had showed me about through a vision in West Virginia. In the meantime, things were not going well at the church.

Mr. Lens had expanded his business everywhere in the building; it had become a serious problem. I remember on a special occasion Jael and her friend had come to be part of the service. Mitchell and I led the service that night and Jael was the guest speaker, but before she preached her message that night she gave a word to Mitchell and she told him that the Lord was going to open many doors for us. She had no idea how much we were strengthened and encouraged in the Lord, because the devil had sought to afflict us through these three preachers, but God had delivered us through His word. It was very encouraging.

Jael preached a powerful message, and we had a Holy Ghost meeting that night. However, there were some critics already going on about the way she had delivered the message. It might have been a gender-related issue, because one of the three preachers didn't believe in female preachers. The word of God tells me that there is neither male nor female in the body of Christ, for we are all one in Him (Galatians 3:28). God chooses whom He will to carry out His word.

The revival was supposed to go on for 90 days, but the way things were going Mitchell and I already knew what was going to happen. Mr. Lens didn't want us in the building anymore; that's why he caused all the confusion around us. There was so much confusion in that building that it had become a stench to God's nostrils.

I remember on a specific night of the revival, the three preachers came to start trouble again. After the service was over that night Mitchell called one of the preachers, the main one in charge, and he told him if they could come together in peace and be in one mind and one accord with us, then it was better for them not to even come anymore and be part of this revival. He replied and said, "All right, I reckon me and my people will pull out today." We have not seen them since.

It was June 2013 when it all took place and everything was back to normal, but the church was empty again. I would rather have the peace of God than to have a church filled with people of the wrong spirit. The devil is a liar. Mr. Lens had rejected the ones whom God had sent. Allow me to rephrase this again — he didn't really reject us, but he rejected the Lord.

How can anyone reject the one who gave you life, the One who has suffered and died for our sins on the cross? I will repeat the same words which one of the thieves said to Jesus when he was hung upon the cross: "Lord, remember me when thou comest into thy kingdom." Jesus said unto him, "Verily I say unto thee, today you shall be with me in paradise," (Luke 23:42-43). Dear readers, today is your day. Jesus is alive and well forevermore and He's waiting to start a relationship with you today. Will you answer His call? Jesus loves you with an everlasting love. His love will never fail. Jesus said in Revelation 22:7, "Behold, I come quickly: blessed is he that keepeth the sayings of the prophecy of this book." Not only this book, but the entire word of God: read it, meditate on it, apply it to your heart and at the end it shall speak.

As for Mr. Lens, he kept his business going in the building and could've cared less if we had to end the revival that day. We had been praying and waiting upon an answer from the Lord. On the 70th day of the revival, the Lord spoke to Mitchell and told him to terminate the revival. Mitchell called Mr. Lens and he told him that the Lord had given him some instructions about the revival. Now, Mr. Lens was probably concerned about what the Lord had said concerning the church and he invited Mitchell to his office so he could hear about the instructions.

After Mitchell had told him that the revival had drawn to an end, he looked at him and said, "Me and you good?"

Mitchell said, "Yes, we are."

After Mitchell had walked out of his office, he called out and said, "Do you need a ride?"

Mitchell said, "No, but me and the Lord will walk out of here."

It's funny how the world could care less about the works of God, but God cares for them. That's the kind of God that I serve. However, there comes a time when we all have to stand in front of the judgment throne of God to give account for everything that we have done. The Bible talks about Heaven and Hell, but they are two different paths. The one path leads to life, while the other one leads to death, that is eternal separation from God. Choose God and live...God also said that He didn't create Hell for His children, but it was prepared for Satan and his angels.

In Revelation 21:8, it talks about how the fearful and unbelieving, and the abominable, and murderers, and whoremongers, and sorcerers, and idolaters, and all liars shall have their part in Hell. We have a decision to make. God wants us to choose life and not death. God never intended for any of His children to go to this place. If we decide not to walk according to the word of God, then we make our own choice to avoid Heaven and go to that place which is eternal separation from God.

I remember right after we closed the revival, we went through a long period of sufferings. Nobody but God knew the trial that we were going through inside of our small place. Because we didn't own a vehicle, it made our trial harder on us. Even the landlord was against us because her heart wasn't right with God.

2 Timothy 2:12 says if we suffer with Jesus, we shall also reign with Him. For those of you right now who are going through diverse trials and tribulations, be encouraged and know that the God you serve will deliver you and bring you out from all of your trials and adversities. Haggai 2:9 says, "The glory of this latter house shall be greater than of the former, saith the Lord of hosts. And in this place will I give peace, saith the Lord of hosts." In the end, you and I will give glory and praise to the Lord just like Job did.

Remember how Job had lost everything, but in the end God gave him double for his trouble. Our trials come not to destroy us, but to mold us and make us stronger in God so that we can save many lives. I remember Joseph told his brothers in Genesis 50:20 "But as for you, ye thought evil against me, but God meant it unto good, to bring to pass, as it is this day, to save much people alive."

What the Lord is saying right now to you and I is this: Rejoice and be glad, for what the enemy meant for evil, God will turn it around for your Good... Hallelujah, praise the Lord in this place! I thank the Lord for our trials, although they seem so unfair and very harsh, but I know that God has a plan for both you and me. It is a plan to prosper you and not to harm you; plans to give you hope and a future. (Jeremiah 29:11).

God will see you through

The last thing that happened to both of us was in the beginning of December 2013. Mitchell had a stroke, but he wasn't aware of it. I knew something was wrong with him, but I couldn't really tell what it was. The next morning when we woke up, I noticed he couldn't speak well. He had a loss of speech. The same morning the Lord sent a friend of ours named Molly to our place. She immediately noticed that there was something wrong with Mitchell and she suggested taking him to the hospital. She took us to the hospital and after the doctors had examined him, they took his blood pressure. It was 238/122 and he was immediately admitted in the hospital for 4 days.

After the doctors had performed many tests on him, they told him if he had not come to the hospital when he did, he could have died. I respect the doctor's sayings and all, and I commend all the doctors out there for doing a great work and for saving many lives, but there comes a time when you're dealing with a sickness that is beyond human reasoning, and then the Lord proves Himself. I remember upon our last day in the hospital, the Lord visited us.

At 2 am a vision came to me. In my vision there were 12 of us, including Mitchell, praying in a room in one mind and in one accord, and after we had stopped praying, I heard the Lord telling us to keep praying. We continued to pray again the second time, and I noticed that the atmosphere around us began to shift, but then we stopped. The Lord said the third time to keep praying. When we continued to pray the third time, something great happened. In my spirit I felt the power of God come in like a mighty whirlwind, and it picked up all of us who were in the room that night and transported us to another place.

When I came to myself in the vision, I saw all twelve of us on top of a high building in a strange country. We were the only ones awake in that place. I spoke up and said, "Do you guys realize what just happened to us?" One moment we were in a room praying, and the next minute we found ourselves on top of a great building in a strange country. I said to them "We've just had an upper room experience."

A man who wasn't one of us came out of nowhere and confirmed the word that I had just spoken to the people and he said, "Yes, that's what happened in the upper room;" and he was gone.

After I woke up from the vision I looked at the clock and it was 2:30 am, but even as I was waking up out of sleep the power of God was present in the hospital room. The Lord touched Mitchell that night, which is why he was healed and made whole within a month. My Lord and my God, what power!

The great move of God in the supernatural is here, but God is looking for a people who hunger and thirst after His righteousness to pour out His power and His spirit upon them. I care more about God's report, for He is the greatest physician. He told Mitchell that He has a ministry to fulfill in him; therefore I know what happened to Mitchell was a test. The Lord told us that He has put us together for the ministry.

I'm telling you, God performed a miracle through him within a month. He is whole! He speaks plainly, and he can move around on his own. If you see him now you would never know that he had a stroke. I can testify that Mitchell is a walking miracle, because we serve a great God who is able to break down and also able to build back up. God said He sent His word to heal our diseases and He is the Lord who heals us in body, soul, and spirit (Exodus 15:26). Remember Isaiah 53:5 says, "But he was wounded for our transgressions, he was bruised for our iniquities: the chastisement of our peace was upon him; and by his stripes we are healed." I thank Hospital of Faith and staff for performing the first aid on my husband. They have done a remarkable job and I commend them for it; God bless them all.

Jesus loves you with an everlasting love and He is waiting on you to come back to him because He is your first love. Jesus says in John 14:6, "I am the way, the truth, and the life: no man cometh unto the father, but by me."

CONTACT US:

Whirlwind Crossfire Ministries
Email: m.jeffers650@gmail.com
guerline_c@hotmail.com

WORDS OF ENCOURAGMENT

If you have experienced any fear in your life, read 2 Timothy 1:7: "For God hath not given you the spirit of fear; but of power, and of love, and of a sound mind."

If the devil is messing with your mind and telling you that you can't do anything, read Philippians 4:13: "I can do all things through Christ who strengthened me."

If your enemy is telling you that you're not strong enough to make it, read 1 John 4:4: "Ye are of God little children, and have overcome them: because greater is he that is in you, than he that is in the world."

INVITATION TO SALVATION

If you haven't yet received Jesus as your personal Savior...today is your day! Repeat this prayer right where you are: Dear Lord Jesus, I repent of my sins. Thank you for dying on the cross for me. I believe you are the Son of God. Come into my heart. I accept you as the Lord and Savior of my life today, in Jesus' name, Amen.

www.ingramcontent.com/pod-product-compliance
Lightning Source LLC
LaVergne TN
LVHW041712060526
838201LV00043B/692